Praise for
Demystifying Fundraising Funnels

"Every non-profit organization should follow the principles in this book, especially in today's current climate where fundraising has become trickier. The book shows you step-by-step how to successfully run online fundraising campaigns so you can grow your organization faster and help more people."

—Corinna Essa, Author of *Money on Demand* and *Reach*

"*Demystifying Fundraising Funnels* is literally the utmost, thoroughly comprehensive, easy to read and understand, "Step by Step" manual in effectively preparing the novice through a seasoned and experienced non-profit fundraiser. This manual also serves as an empathetic and dynamic game-changer and resource for "grassroots and inner-city" organizations attempting to lay foundational roots within the many times biased cultural and racial arena of fundraising. It receives my highest praise!"

—V. Derek Morris Doctoral Candidate, Social Justice Innovation and Change, University of Southern California Suzanne Dworak-Peck School of Social Work

"We just completed a major capital campaign for our church and are embarking on one for our school. David's research, insight, tools, and their application are timely and much needed in the new landscape of fundraising."

—Pastors Phil & Kari Vance, Senior Pastors of Living Faith Fellowship, Pullman, WA

"One overriding theme that my work with for-profits and non-profits is that the non-profit world needs to adopt "real world" online marketing tools.
"Demystifying Fundraising Funnels provides the most direct methods to grow your donor and grant revenues. It is a must-read for both staff and boards of directors."

—Dr. Allan Colman, Author of *The Success Accelerator*

"*Demystifying Fundraising Funnels* provides a practical guide on how fundraising funnels can help non-profit leadership increase their contributions with a step-by-step approach to develop a plan. In addition, Higgins includes a wide range of supportive statistics on the subject, suggesting thoughtful questions and highlighting relatable case studies."

—Jeanne E. Schmelzer, CFRE, Executive Vice President, Netzel Grigsby Associates

"Higgins gives us an empathic perspective that is structured. He allows the reader to take steps in engaging goals related to non-profit organizations. He combines the insights or down-to-earth "push up your sleeves" hard work with developed aspects of technology and the direction of the future. Higgins provides real-life transparency reflecting his resilience after learning from mistakes. This is an exceptional manner of encouragement based on the marriage of years and thorough analysis."

—Howard Morrison, Attorney at Law, Child Advocate

"For nearly 50 years, we have served in non-profit organizations both nationally and internationally. Yet, funding is the constant crying challenge. David's book, *Demystifying Fundraising Funnels*, is the answer to that call. If you implement his information in your business, you will well provide for those you serve."

—Bill Burkhardt, Coach, Speaker, Author, Fathers Heart Ministry

"In a world where a million voices are competing for your donor's time, attention, and resources – fundraising becomes complicated. David brings simple clarity to non-profits on how not to become lost in all the noise. There is a whole community of people who resonate with your mission, ideals, and goals. This is the handbook on how to find them."

—Robert Pugh, Senior Fraud Investigator, Communications Professional, Non-profit Fundraiser Strategist

"In the many years that I have known him, David Higgins has always demonstrated a deep passion for seeing other people thrive. *Demystifying Fundraising Funnels* reflects that same heart, and I am certain that any Individual, Ministry, and Non-profit organization will do very well to follow the principles detailed in this ground-breaking work."

—Craig Kruse, Lead Pastor, South Coast Church

"If your non-profit is on life support - You need to adapt or die!" "*Demystifying Fundraising Funnels* is designed for the non-profit of the twenty-first century that needs to raise funds in a new world of social media platforms. David introduces you to digital marketing strategies and secrets that you must know to be successful. The critically important, practical information, insight, and inspiration in this book will help you build and fund a vision for the future."

—Dr. Henry Wolmarans D.Min., Ph.D., CEO The Promise Nonprofit Inc., Author of *Financial Guide for Believers*

"A must-read if you are running a non-profit! David opened my eyes to the new age of digital fundraising. If I had this information five years ago, it would have changed everything for our organization. So don't just put this in your reading queue; put it at the top of your list."

—Charles "Tim" Geisler, Nonprofit Director/ Retired, Washington Licensed Realtor

"I can't express enough how helpful this book was to me. It has answered many questions I have right now. *Demystifying Fundraising Funnels* truly lives up to the title. This book is insightful, practical, and relevant to the times. This is a must-read for non-profits."

—Scott Ingegneri, Founder of Awaken Ministries Int'l

"David has done a masterful job of communicating the need for non-profits to be rethinking their current fundraising strategies. Through others' testimonies, his personal stories, strategies, and practical application. David takes you by the hand and leads you into the next digital frontier for effective fundraising!"

—Mike Lindell, Lead Pastor, One Life Family Worship

"Can I say WOW? What a timely book and resource for non-profits everywhere. David draws on his extensive experience in both the non-profit and business worlds and gives non-profits a road map on how to face the new and always changing challenges that come with fundraising. This resource is full of amazing insight, current stats, and guided assessments so that fundraising becomes lightweight and low maintenance as your organization reaches for its dreams."

—Mike "Mookie" Cunningham, HK Ventures LLC, Co-Owner and Operator

"This exciting new book is one every non-profit should follow. Let David be your guide to limitless possibilities; it is an absolute game-changer!"

—Brady Augustine, CNE, Berkshire Hathaway HSNW RE

"Having been in leadership within non-profit organizations since 1985, I can unabashedly recommend *Demystifying Fundraising Funnels*. As a former Executive Director, I was so busy running the organization that I thought I didn't have time to raise the needed funds effectively. This book would have been a godsend, and I am confident it will be just that for all who take the time to read it."

—Dawn Golladay, Nonprofit Executive Director, Retired

"I found this book a breakthrough event for understanding how a non-profit of any size can use digital marketing to its fullest advantage. So take the plunge and challenge yourself and your staff to move into the digital fundraising world."

—Trisha Gooch, Development Consultant

"In reviewing his work of "demystifying" the realm of fundraising in this digital age, I found this book to be precise and to the point! Its most compelling feature is that it is very user-friendly. I highly recommend his work to all non-profit organizations."

—Rev. Tim Pounds, Lead Pastor

DEMYSTIFYING FUNDRAISING FUNNELS

DEMYSTIFYING FUNDRAISING FUNNELS

A Digital Marketing Blueprint to Fund Your Non-Profit

DAVID HIGGINS

MADE FOR
SUCCESS

Made for Success Publishing
P.O. Box 1775 Issaquah, WA 98027
www.MadeForSuccessPublishing.com

Distributed by Made for Success Publishing
First Printing

Library of Congress Cataloging-in-Publication data
Higgins, David
    Demystifying Fundraising Funnels: A Digital Marketing Blueprint
    to Fund Your Non-Profit
        p. cm.

LCCN: 2021950976
ISBN: 978-1-64146-692-9 (*Paperback*)
ISBN: 978-1-64146-693-6 (*eBook)*
ISBN: 978-1-64146-694-3 (*Audiobook)*

Printed in the United States of America

For further information contact Made for Success Publishing
+14255266480 or email service@madeforsuccess.net

CONTENTS

BECAUSE OF YOU,
THESE WORDS ARE HERE

*To my father, who instilled in me the love of nonprofits
and the amazing people who serve them.
To my mum, who always communicated
with kindness and hope.*

*To my amazing wife Michelle, who
has supported me through so many crazy ideas
and has been my partner in dreaming and building.*

*To my incredible children, who
have always been my cheer squad,
brainstorming ideas and investing
many smiles, hugs, and time with
nonprofits around the world.*

PREFACE

So … you want to find hundreds or even thousands of new donors for your organization? They are out there, waiting to learn that your nonprofit exists. You just need to connect with them. That is what this book is about. This is the how. How do you, as an overworked and growing 501(c), reach your funding goals and, heaven forbid, exceed them? What could you do with a 20% or more increase in your income?

Each of us has a unique journey. You learn from your past experiences and, through them, make decisions that impact your present and future. It is my goal to share with you what I have learned in digital marketing and translate it into the language of nonprofits.

Can you increase your horizons and the possibilities of what may be? By learning about and acting upon what I am sharing with you, online digital marketing funnel systems, you will discover that this is how revenue is exchanging hands today. You will see that monetary exchange is being initiated online in product funnels, and your nonprofit needs to be able to engage within this economic system.

It's time to start building new email-attraction funnels, donation funnels, and influencer-driven funnels, then create e-commerce funnels, fundraiser-driver funnels, and attendance funnels. This new language in the world of nonprofit income is going to "lift the lid" on your revenue and engage programs your nonprofit has needed to launch for some time.

My aim is to provide a blueprint so your nonprofit can strategize its online engagement in the emerging and extremely exciting world of digital nonprofit funding. It's a world that goes beyond websites and into funnel building and the drivers that are used for their success. Not only will you see why things are changing and what they have become, but also how to begin your journey.

What This Book Does Not Promise

You will NOT be promised a quick income system that will solve all your problems. But within this discussion on digitally driven nonprofit donor discovery tools and donation funnels, you will see how others have used a simple and easily reproducible way to build their bottom line and greatly increase annual revenue.

You will NOT be told this is a guarantee to increase your organization's popularity and fan base. But I will share stories of how many nonprofit organizations use the tools adopted from highly profitable digital marketing companies to raise hundreds of thousands of dollars (and in a few cases, millions of dollars), as well as create a national and international voice.

It is one thing to understand the principles communicated and a vastly different one to feel they are a guarantee of your own success. Each journey has unique struggles and frustrations that can alter outcomes. However, through education, understanding, and brave first attempts, you can increase your chance of success between failure and success. Whenever you learn something new, you must expect a growth curve: from the state of curiosity into a state of first attempts; from the first attempts into skills of competence; and from there into mastery, where true impact is felt.

Discovering the principles and connection to the micro-community around you (those within your current arena of relationship and influence), as well as the macro-community (those who share your interest nationally and across borders), can change the power and reach of your voice. As you read this, consider the "whom" you would like to influence within the scope of your nonprofit's direction.

If you are in a battle with confidence, you will learn how others emerged from positions like yours and changed the outcomes for themselves and their organizations. You will see how their strategies and tactics worked for them and recreate them for your own unique situations.

My team and I are here to aid you in discovering ways through these tensions of your organization. With the tools provided and layered communication we make available to you, my hope is that this read, and the outcome from your time spent, will result in breakthroughs for you and your organization.

This book will help you get started and introduce you to the tools of the digital Nonprofit Funnel Builder and the excitement of becoming part of the "nonprofit online" community.

Let's get started!

INTRODUCTION

IN A BOARDROOM NEAR YOU

"Great things are done by a series of small things brought together."
—Vincent Van Gogh

"Team! We need a solid strategy to find new donors and fund our upcoming year!" John exclaimed to his board. "We rely too highly on grants. If we lose one grant, we have to cut staff and programs. We need to find new individual donors. How are we going to do that?"

As John looked around the table, he halted his gaze at Darnell and Colin.

"Where are we after last night's funding dinner?"

"Well…" Darnell paused, gathering his words. "After 7 months of planning, and with a budget of $550,000, we were able to raise $1.4 million." He reached over to Colin, and they exchanged an elated high five.

"How much did we need to raise?" John asked, looking at the sheet Margaret was handing him.

"$1.9 million," Margaret said, quickly looking over at Darnell.

John squeezed his eyes shut and mumbled, "We're $500,000 short of making goal this year. This is why we need to find an answer to my question."

"Have you heard of digital marketing funnels being used by nonprofits?" Margaret quietly asked. "Charity: Water raised hundreds of millions in the last few years, and online social media and marketing funnels have driven that number. There's also this children's program director guy up in Ottawa, Canada, who was trying to keep his summer camp open a few years back. In his first year of turning a digital sales funnel into a nonprofit email-attraction funnel, he added 300 kids to his camp. And he was just figuring it out. Last year, he raised over $1 million with only one marketing funnel."

Scoffing, Colin said, "That's unbelievable. He must have been a tech guy. And what's a kid camp in Canada going to do with a million bucks?"

Margaret quickly typed in the web address she found that morning and spun the laptop around so the group could see it. Looking right back at Colin, she responded, "This Tylor guy didn't know much and didn't have a big team.[a] It was mostly just he and his wife." Smiling, she continued. "Oh, and they spent the extra money expanding the camp so they could help more kids."

"That's it!" John exclaimed. "Let's figure out what these online digital marketing funnels are and put them to work ASAP."

CHAPTER 1

A DIGITAL MARKETING BLUEPRINT FOR NONPROFITS

"Desire is a treasure map. Knowledge is the treasure chest. Wisdom is the jewel. Yet, without action, they all stay buried."

—Unknown

You are surrounded by amazing nonprofit organizations that are desperately needed in their communities. Unfortunately, they are most likely knocking at death's door—and they don't even know it.

While current fundraising methods date back to 1920-1940 and use antiquated marketing techniques, the economy is shifting, and the way money is exchanged has changed. The effectiveness of such fundraisers is waning, and they are no longer producing the results needed for our nonprofits to keep growing. The truth is, in the next decade, many desperately needed 501(c)s are going to fade away for one reason: They did not pivot to online fundraising.

In 2020, COVID-19 got its hooks into the economy and impacted nonprofits around the globe. Because of the lockdowns and most nonprofits' reliance on what I call tactile or "physical" fundraising, income dropped dramatically for those not creating new online funding sources. Many nonprofits fell into crisis. The question many started to wrestle with was, "How can my nonprofit thrive in this emerging online economy?"

When I see the incredible resources created by groups like Untapped Shores and their drive to bring clean water to African villages, or Heart of Camden using donation funnels to create community connections and funding, I can confidently say, "Yes, it can be done."

Where Did My Journey Begin?

At first it started with hunches. I was buying another item I didn't really need on Amazon when I started seeing the pattern. I had the audacity to think I was in control of the buying journey, but I noticed that as soon as I typed in what I was looking for, I was susceptible to their suggestions and value increases. By the time I logged out, feeling as if I had just received an amazing product and received a whole lot of other great value because of my amazing timing in making the purchase, it hit me.

Amazon had led me right where I wanted to go.

I had entered a digital marketing funnel and felt great at the other end.

The next evening, I was on TikTok, and an advertisement for "state of the art earbuds" popped up. The ad was designed to be seen, read, and acted upon in 3.2 seconds and quickly grabbed my attention. It was a completely emotional sales ad "driver." As soon as I touched the ad link, I was in a sales funnel. I clicked the buy link and was immediately offered a second set for 50% off. *What a deal!* Of course, I needed a second set, and for such a great deal, I could give a pair to my wife. I was then asked if I wanted three other things that people who bought the earbuds also purchased. The answer was "nope," and I was let out of the funnel with a big thank you and a smile. Then it happened to me again. The same pattern.

Oberlo.com states 2.14 billion people worldwide are shopping online. What's the total world population, you may ask?[1]

So, I started throwing myself into research. If this was happening in the worldwide economy, and the exchange of revenue was shifting so quickly from brick-and-mortar to online, what was happening for nonprofits? What was our response to this shift in the exchange of revenue?

I reached out on LinkedIn, requesting interviews from hundreds of nonprofit leaders. In my research, I started finding charities that were successfully using digital online fundraising for themselves, and another new pattern started to show itself.

All over the U.S. and Canada, there were independent organizations that had moved beyond previously used methods of raising income and had started implementing and re-designing digital marketing techniques. In the middle of a pandemic, when no one was able to shake a hand, meet at a donor dinner, have a concert, or organize a 5K run, some nonprofits were over budget. Yes, *over* budget!

I set out to learn what they were doing that was working so well, and a blueprint began to emerge. My hunches became backed by facts, and a repeatable framework became clear. I had found online marketing practices that, if carefully implemented and managed, nonprofits could reap for incredible results. I created my own easily accessible blueprint that would open the door for any nonprofit willing to upskill and learn how to exchange value for revenue.

From a small, inner-city nonprofit in San Francisco helping the homeless to the suicide prevention hotline in Oklahoma City, it worked. From the urban dance group in Los Angeles to the Food Pantry in Philadelphia, it worked. My friends in Lucknow, India, and Mazabuka, Zambia, could find success with it. Someone in Vanuatu with a computer and a hunger to upskill could create the same nonprofit fundraising outcomes as a trade-skills training nonprofit in Auckland, New Zealand, or Sydney, Australia.

It comes down to one basic question: Can you retool, reimagine, and relaunch? Can this growing funding channel create a movement of people such as yourself to open up the digital tools and find new funding and relationships with an emerging, powerful generation of donors? Would you be willing to take advantage of skills, programs, and systems birthed in the digital marketing workplace to take your institutional funding online?

WORKING IT OUT

Three Questions

How would I rate my nonprofit's online presence?

☐ Extremely effective
☐ Effective
☐ Somewhat effective
☐ Not effective

How many donors are gained from our online activities?

A. In the last 12 months: _____
B. In the next 12 months if we don't change: _____
C. In the next 12 months with ideal change: _____

What is the income raised from all online sources?

A. In the last 12 months: _____
B. Ideally in the next 12 months: _____

CHAPTER 2

DISCOVERING THE NEW DONOR CULTURE

"The world is moving so fast that the person who says it can't be done is generally interrupted by someone doing it."
—Elbert Hubbard

As the director of donor events for the San Francisco Museum of Modern Art, Cimeron was buzzing with excitement. She had assembled an amazing showcase hosted by museums around the city that would open their doors for one evening only. The 2017 "Art Bash" was the fundraising event of the year. Nine months of preparation and hundreds of thousands of dollars had been spent on decor, entertainment, marketing, and enticing celebrities to bring this night to life. At the end of the night (and with a multitude of happy donors), the museum grossed well over a million dollars.

Just a few years later in the depths of the pandemic, Cimeron left the nonprofit world and accepted an exceptional offer from a cutting-edge marketing firm. Soon after we met, she shared some acute changes she had faced before leaving the museum.

"The fundamentals of fundraising are changing," she said. "There used to be established donors who wanted their names on the building, but they are all in their 80s now. Then their children began to inherit the family fortune, but they don't look at the long term and have different values than the previous generations. Their homes are international, and they don't want to be committed for more than one year."

Research confirms that classic nonprofit fundraising is no longer enough. The next generation of donors is unlike any who have come before, and you need to connect to them via a new language.

Are Nonprofits the Next RadioShack?

I remember when RadioShack and Kmart were the go-to places if I wanted to buy a Walkman when I was a kid. Then people started to realize that everything at RadioShack and Kmart could be found on Amazon. When store sales began to slide, I imagined the conversation in the corporate boardroom meeting. "There will always be a place for the storefront."

In the mid-2000s, RadioShack and Kmart woke up to find their stores empty. Websites were quickly built, but the shopping process was clunky. Society had pivoted, and they hadn't pivoted with it quickly enough.

Many much-needed, impactful nonprofits are sliding toward the same unfortunate demise because they haven't changed with the societal shifts. Those who are just beginning to understand the change and only make a halfhearted shift will certainly face the same fate as RadioShack and Kmart.

Enter Digital Marketing Funnels

Five years ago, a new change hit the marketplace. People had slowly stopped going to websites to search and shop and started allowing search algorithms to bring exact products to them. Now the store web domain is more of a *brochure* for the business, while real revenue is being produced through product "sales funnels" and upselling after the sale.

Walmart recognized this early and, following Amazon's lead, has modified its online store to compete with Amazon. The two online giants' websites now function like the aforementioned sales funnel.

For example, you run across an ad that matches a search you recently initiated or a conversation with a friend that was picked up on your cellphone. (Yes, they are listening.) Because it's relevant to your current need, you click on the picture or ad for the single product. Suddenly, you are on a single product sales site with the option to upgrade to a larger or higher-quality item. When you decide to check out and pay, you are told, "Others who bought this product also purchased this, or this, or this."

This is a classic funnel

Next, you are offered a one-time offer: "Click here to get 15% off this sale by applying for our credit card. FREE for 30 days." (Shhh… and only 26% interest after all.) That was the upsell.

You filled out the "quick" credit card application, didn't you? That's alright, I did, too.

What had happened in the early 2000s with the "product sales" websites started to become relevant to nonprofits almost five years later, and nonprofits started seeing the power of their website to drive funding and community connection. By 2005, a nonprofit without a vibrant website was sliding into obscurity. Just a short decade later, we see this happening again. The year 2016 was the beginning of the online sales funnel boom. Now we're pushing past five years later, and online funnels are mature and ready for nonprofits.

We historically used marketing flyers and newsletters for our nonprofits; we advertised in phone directories and newspapers. Then, as transition caused us to take a turn, we were pushed into website development and training our staff to use phone campaigns.

As marketing has changed with the times, so has the necessity for nonprofits to pivot into the next technology that is engaging the population. That's where we will find our next generation of donors, and that is why we find ourselves considering how to use digital marketing funnel templates and repurposing them for community engagement and funding drives.

What's Next?

I hear you wondering, "What's the next change for buyers? What's the next shift in market-driven communication?"

We are still about five years away from the next big shift, and another few beyond that before it will be strongly impacting us as nonprofits. The answer to the above question, I believe, is in the language of the internet and its acceptance of "blockchain" technology.

In the meantime, let's focus on the art and skillsets of building amazing email attraction funnels and donation funnel campaigns and allowing the speed and programs within digital marketing to do the work of dozens of our volunteers.

Let's strategize vibrant email-attraction funnels to introduce your organization to millions of potential donors and begin the relationships that will raise lots of funding for your next programs.

How Easy is it to Find New Donors?

If you ask the birdwatcher who is standing in Washington state how easy it is to find an African fish eagle, the answer is near impossible. But if you are in the sub-Saharan region of Africa, you'll find them easily. What I'm saying is, you need to go to where the donors are, or create an environment of such value the donors will leave their comfort zone to come to you.

So, where are your future donors?

Nine out of ten Americans are communicating through email, and 50% worldwide are daily checking their email. In fact, email generates <u>$42 for every $1 spent</u>, which is an astounding 4,200% ROI, making it one of the most effective options available.[2]

Currently, more than half (53%) of the global population use social media, which is a 12.3% year-over-year increase.[3]

According to the latest official data, Instagram has 1 billion monthly active users (MAUs) globally, with 130 million users in the United States alone.[4]

TikTok users open their account 8 times every day.[5] The U.S. audience is now over 100 million. The U.S. population, in the second I typed this onto my page, is 332,569,415. That means in your city, 1 out of 3 people are logging onto TikTok, and it is now available in 154 countries worldwide. This data comes straight from TikTok.

E-commerce, as an industry, did not exist 30 years ago. Now it is the largest mover of finance in the history of global economics. The North

American e-commerce market is worth just under $912 billion and is growing at a rate of 13% a year.[6]

David Williams of RJMetrics reported their finding in the "2015 Ecommerce Growth Benchmark Report."[7] They studied 200+ ecommerce businesses, 31 million customers, and $25 billion in transactions "…at three months the average e-commerce site is generating just over $150,000 in monthly revenue by the end of year one.

"By year two, businesses are averaging almost $330,000 in monthly revenue. After three years, they're bringing in over $1 million in revenue every month, an increase of over 230% between year one and year three. On average, an e-commerce site has generated over $20 million in revenue by the end of year three in business."

In 2020, Digital Commerce 360 reported that 21.3% of money that was exchanged was using "U.S. Ecommerce rather than Retail Stores."[8] American consumers are quickly shifting to using online sites and funnels as their premier source of revenue exchange.

What can you learn from this data? First, your community is online, and that is the premier way of connecting and starting new relationships. Second, your donor language is a digital one. Either you learn to speak their language, or you will never attract their ear. Third, pivot or die. Your nonprofit needs to embrace the pain to upskill and learn this new language or become more and more irrelevant and eventually close your doors.

If your nonprofit vision is to thrive and meet the needs built into your purpose, then you need to act now.

A Small Test Study

We did a study of 96 501(c)s in Yakima Valley, WA, an area with a population of approximately 150,000. Three out of four of these nonprofits had an active, well-built website, but 15% had only a Facebook page, mostly out of date. Of a dozen directors we spoke to, only three were active on any social media platform, and none were even interested in TikTok.

Of the two boards of directors we spoke to, only one individual person had a Facebook page. When asked about how often they sent emails, the few who were active admitted it was a weekly informational email for the members only.

Statistically, what does this tell you about this small study group?

First, outside of the core group already online, not one of our test cases was communicating to the whole Yakima Valley population. This was confirmed when four different directors said, "Most of our new volunteers come from other charity groups in the Valley." They had become completely insular.

Second, the 501(c)s were not speaking the language of the community. Whether the community was curious about the mission or wanted to find a like-minded community member to connect to, or just wanted to know how to donate, there was no online connection happening with the local population.

Third, there were no staff members tasked with strategic online social networking that involved the community.

If a board of directors, with foresight, hired a skilled person to lead the charge, they would soon find that person skillfully using marketing funnels, not only raising the funds needed for their own salary, but creating more funds, future committed donors, and volunteers falling in love with the mission of the nonprofit.

Nearly every nonprofit in this test group had put aside some money for community connections, but only for flyers, door-to-door fundraising, or physical fundraising events to attract the neighborhood. These types of marketing techniques were mostly adopted from tactics created by marketing companies from 1920-1940.

Only 13 of them had budgeted for digital communication, e.g., their website, and of that group, only 3 were within 10 years of relevance in their visuals and text on their domain. None were running digital marketing funnels of any kind or had a strategy to use email attraction or donation funnels.

We determined that 5 were totally invisible and publicly nonfunctioning; 32 were 100% invisible within the community; 46 were obsolete and within a few years of being irrelevant or closed. Only 10 were communicating in a manner that facilitated interested people (typically ages 55 and older) in finding their website. And only 3 were actively trying to speak to the community through digital means.

We could conclude that within 10 years, probably 60%-80% of these nonprofits (unless funded directly by a trust or focused grants), because of lack of new donors and funding, would no longer be able keep their doors open.

How can nonprofits turn this around? The first step is knowing there is an effective solution, and it's not that difficult. You could hire outside help, but it is not necessary. A nonprofit will need to upskill and invest in new tools, but that is not as daunting as it may at first seem.

Now we address the question above: how do we find new donors? We start attracting donors through value creation. We want to provide something, often information, that will benefit donors. Second, you will need to provide a tool donors can easily find and use that will create a positive online "handshake." We will talk about this more in the next chapter.

Another Case Study

A notable nonprofit that has done this well is Charity: Water (charitywater. org). I first ran into Charity: Water a couple of years ago when searching nonprofit fundraising on YouTube. They were all over the platform. They were communicating in the language society was speaking.

When I looked them up on Facebook, I was dropped right into a funnel. Go on TikTok and Instagram, put in #chaitywater and boom! Another funnel. After I searched for them, guess what started showing up on my feeds? Charity: Water invites/ads that escorted me to another donation funnel.

In 14 years, with the help of more than 1 million supporters worldwide,[9] Charity: Water has raised over $539 million and funded over 64,000 water projects in 29 countries. When completed, those projects will provide over 12.6 million people with clean, safe drinking water.

What is important to understand is that donors are out there in the millions. The tools are available. The education is quickly accessible. Now is the time to immerse your nonprofit in the new donor culture and language.

WORKING IT OUT

Three Questions

How frequently are my staff and I on social media?

Me: □ Daily □ Multiple □ Just for occasional
times a week updates?

My staff: □ Daily □ Multiple □ Just for occasional
times a week updates?

How many times per month do we update our website and check it for attractiveness? _____

Review six websites in the same niche as your nonprofit and do a side-by-side comparison.

A. What is the first emotion that the color and home page evokes?

_____

Ideas: Hope, serious, happy, passionate, confused, life, struggle, info, boring

B. Is there an engaged, happy person on the opening page or a color, symbol, building, or a person under duress? _____

C. Is there an easily seen DONATE button on the first page?

_____

CHAPTER 3

BRIDGING THE COMMUNICATION GAP BY USING THE RIGHT LANGUAGE AND DRIVERS

"Your problem is to bridge the gap that exists between where you are now and the goal you intend to reach."
—Earl Nightingale

How do you speak to the new generation? What is the language that will allow you to attract the online donor to your cause? This is what we will cover in these next chapters.

Bethany said to me as we dove into her nonprofit experience and frustrations, "I'm 57, and my board is mostly over the age of 60. We are just not relevant anymore to the millennial or online donor. It seems impossible to think we will be able to transition a portion of our funding to online funnels."

As I shared with Bethany, the beautiful thing about funnels is your communication is in words. If you can learn the language of the readers, you can connect to their hearts. Funnels do not care about your age or the age of your board. Funnels do not judge you because of your associations, friends, skin color, or neighborhood. They are a tool, and the wording for nonprofits has only two rules:

1. Be truthful.
2. Be kind.

Let's have language lessons that will allow introverts and extroverts to be equally successful. If you are in Bethany's shoes, these five language lessons will give you the chance to broaden your reach and look beyond your face-to-face limitations.

Language Lesson #1: Identify Your Ideal Donor

Who is the most likely person to donate to you? If your organization focuses on elderly care, you may want to focus on Gen Xers whose parents would be in that service range. We also know women are more likely to donate than men. Then, consider if marriage and children are factors, as well as income levels.

We would then create a composite of the ideal donor for the Elderly Care Center. Who is she, and how do we reach her? Let's call her Beth. Now, Beth is our ideal donor avatar.

Statistics for Millennials (25-40/yrs. old)

Nonprofits Source states that the largest current group of donors by population is Millennials born between 1981–1996.[10] They are 25.9% of the U.S. population. Here are some hard-hitting numbers that I hope impress you as much as they did me:

- 46% donate to crowdfunding campaigns.
- 16% give through Facebook fundraising tools.
- 64% volunteer locally; 9% internationally.
- 55% attend fundraising events. (Consider how they were invited.)
- 84% of Millennials give to charity, individually donating an annual average of $481 across 3.3 organizations.

- Millennials are active on their phones and respond best to text messages and social media, but rarely check personal email or respond to voice messages.
- Millennials are most likely to contribute to work-sponsored initiatives, donate via mobile devices, and watch online videos before making a gift.
- 47% of Millennials gave through an organization's website in 2016.

Statistics for Generation X (41-56/yrs. old)

Gen Xers were born between 1965–1980 and represent 20.4% of the U.S. population. Though they are wealthier, they are smaller by volume than Millennials. Overall, they can also be more sarcastic… Imagine that?!

- 45% donate to crowdfunding campaigns.
- 19% give through Facebook fundraising tools.
- 64% volunteer locally; 8% internationally.
- 56% attend fundraising events. (Consider how they came to know about the event.)
- Gen Xers are most likely to fundraise on behalf of a cause, make a pledge, and volunteer their time to an organization.
- Gen Xers prefer text messages or voice messages. These donors regularly check email and stay up to date on social media feeds.
- Email prompted 31% of online donations made by Gen Xers.
- 59% are inspired to donate to charity by a message/image they saw on social media.

Statistics for Boomers (57-75/yrs. old)

Baby Boomers were born between 1946–1964. They represent 23.6% of the U.S. population. This is a very generous generation with a lot of wealth that has been acquired. The interesting thing to note is how many of them are building relationships online, shopping online, and engaging in their communities using online tools.

- 35% donate to crowdfunding campaigns.
- 21% give through Facebook fundraising tools.

- 71% volunteer locally; 9% internationally.
- 58% attend fundraising events. (Email is strongly used as a motivator in this age bracket.)
- 72% of Boomers give to charity, donating an annual average of $1,212 across 4.5 organizations.
- Boomers answer voice messages, check email regularly, and also use text messaging and social media. Though initially slow to adopt new technology, they take to it quickly once they do.

Language Lesson #2: Where Do They Gather?

Now that we have identified Beth as our ideal donor, we need to discover where Beth hangs out. What are her network hubs? For those of us who like research, this will be exciting. There are many questions we can ask, and because we have placed Beth as a child of the elderly care niche the nonprofit serves, we start the search for her online connections there.

Just a few months back, I walked a nonprofit I have enjoyed consulting for through this exercise. They are in the boating niche, and we had fun answering this question. Their avatar was Bill and Marsha. We started imagining where they would go to spend their money online and what social networking activities they involved themselves with. Our results looked something like this...

Bill and Marsha shop online for boating equipment at Overton's, West Marine, BoatUS, Defender, Marine, Iboats, Sailboat Stuff, JSI, Sailnet, and Boater's World.

The community chat forums where we could go to hear the questions they are asking and connect to the community they love to spend time with included TheHullTruth, BoatChat, and (just because I love the name) SaltyDogBoatingNews. We also found out there are stores like West Marine that have highly active online boating communities.

What are the sites that the boating community looks to for news, help, and education? An example of one of these is CoastalBoating.

We haven't even scratched the surface, but I would be remiss if I didn't give an "honorable mention" to the thousands of Facebook communities, Instagram and TikTok algorithms, Pinterest, and YouTube channels. There are also Twitch, Twitter, and many other online social networks.

These sites are where our boating avatars Bill and Marsha shop, chat, hang out, and look for news. The nonprofit that wants to engage the boating community can now strategize how to best connect to the people that have the greatest motivation to respond to them. If they want to advertise links to their website or donation funnels, these would be effective places to do so. It's like fishing in a fully stocked lake of hungry bass ready to bite.

Russell Brunson, in one of the best books I have ever read on this subject, *Traffic Secrets*, made this observation: "The real power of the internet is that it has allowed us to connect with like-minded people in a way that wasn't possible before. It's allowed each of us, with our unique and sometimes weird hobbies and interests, to congregate with *our people* to discuss the things that mean the most to us."

We dive into this more in the next chapter.

Language Lesson #3: Use the Right Driver

I was consulting at a social nonprofit earlier this year and asked them what digital marketing funnels they had running. Their response was, "We have a website." I asked what their strategy was to bring people to the website. They said, "We've been looking at getting a 'donate' button put on the site, which a nonprofit Customer Relationship Management (CRM) platform suggested." This is 1998 language.

This is the Kmart dilemma.

Our current generation of donors are not going to type in a domain page, read through your website to discover who you are, find the button to donate, and then finally click it. The average person who is online will stay on a page for five seconds max. My heart hurts every time I hear about a nonprofit asking a CRM company for help and, after spending $1,200 on a website rebuild with a CRM-driven donor button, nothing has changed. They are not attracting any new donors, and funding is down again for another year.

We can't use 1998 and 2005 tools and expect the current generation of donors to see us. Email attraction and donation funnels are brand-new tools for our nonprofit industry, but they have come from a decade of growth and maturing and are very well-designed agents for communication and exchange of revenue.

Here are six ideas that are free "drivers" or portals to connect with new donors:

#1 Start an email drip campaign—a set of relationship-building emails that will be sent out automatically on a schedule.
#2 Do daily Facebook and LinkedIn posts.
#3 Start a podcast or blog or YouTube vlog.
#4 Post 2x/day on Instagram or 6x/day with TikTok.
#5 Join Facebook groups that are communities within your niche.
#6 Join or create chat groups that have to do with your focus.

A driver is a tool used to cause someone to enter your funnel. Here at Nonprofit Online, we have our weekly YouTube vlog. Our YouTube channel is one of the key drivers for our funnels and website. We use it as a tool to bring value to and connect individuals to the message we feel is our mission and purpose. We also have Facebook, LinkedIn, Instagram, and email drivers.

There are also amazingly effective paid ad drivers which, in many cases, allow a larger multiplier, sometimes 10 times more people reached. Once you have your organic drivers in place, and donations are coming in, I strongly encourage you to invest your success in paid ad drivers. If done well with a good strategy, you will find that, for every $1 invested, you can see a $3-$5 return.

Language Lesson #4:
Communicate in Their Language

Summertime was about to arrive, and Ron Couch was prepping his staff and interns for the upcoming series of fundraisers. The goal was to raise several thousands of dollars to get teens to summer camp and send the drama and mime teams to Piccadilly Circus in London, England. As he turned to his team packed into the small classroom, Ron said, "Fundraising season has started, and I want you to come up with ideas that will add value to each fundraiser. Each event needs to net over $1,000 or more. Put your thinking caps on."

His team started to brainstorm ideas. "What if we created a place of connection or community at each event?" Sarah suggested.

"That's good," Ron responded. "What else?"

Everyone just stared at him, so he answered the question himself. "Everyone wants to feel important, and people connect that with, like Sarah said, a sense of community and connection."

This was a great lesson Ron was sharing with these young people, but he was leaving two of the other major motivators out.

Three Core Motivators that Drive Donors

In the book *Expert Secrets*, Russell Brunson writes about the three core markets or desires. A buyer's motivation begins with a feeling of a rise in status wrapped in any of the three following attributes (in no particular order): wealth, health, and relationships.

Dave Johansson, a second-generation nonprofit leader, told me his father spent his life helping charities organize and fundraise. Dave told me his dad described the "big three" giving motivators this way: "65% of donors give because of status; 22% give because of a sense of community; and the rest give out of fear. That's the emotion you wrap around the big three: money, wellbeing, and family." Though these percentages were based on his experience and not a statistically driven survey, very similar conclusions are stated often by marketing professionals[11] thru the years.

These three core motivators, when wrapped around the reasons people give, are the best ways to communicate your mission and needs to donors in a way that will ensure maximum results.

How do you do this? When you're putting together your two-page email attraction funnel, you would use descriptors like the following: "Be a part of our community," or "(Local Celebrity) was here last week and (fill in the blank)." You allow the text or "copy" to communicate through a lens that incorporates one of the big three.

Have you noticed when attending a religious service, and it's time to take up the offering, the person communicating usually speaks about how your tithe/giving is essential to your relationship with the church and/or God? Or it's a seed of faith planted for your healing? Or a direct correlation to increased wealth? "God will give/invest back to you 70 times 7!" The wealthier the religious institution is, the more focused the marketing is on the big three drivers.

The #1 Reason to Donate

This brings us to the best of all drivers. Digital marketing "buyers" can be difficult to reach, but it's different in the nonprofit community. We have a superpower most marketing companies cannot match. More than any other, the greatest reason to donate is love.

Love is the best and healthiest reason to give. If we can teach our donor base the language of giving from love, they will continue funding our organization because they love our purpose and our vision. It's a win/win for everyone. When donors of religious 501(c)3s give because of love in their higher purpose, their donations strengthen in consistency. If the animal shelter can build a core of animal lovers who stand behind them with funding, there is no better donor base. Because their giving is founded in love, it will be loyal.

But in most campaigns, you cannot start at this point. You need to win the attention of your "ideal" donor, then build an email relationship through a drip campaign. Eventually, that sense of connection may release such a sense of unity with your purpose they will start saying things like, "I love what you do!"

But it seldom starts there.

It starts with a basic understanding of the motives behind how people donate vs. buy. What's the difference? There isn't one. Wrapping your organic and paid ad drivers in a language that is influenced by the big three reasons people give will grab the attention of a national audience.

Language Lesson #5: Give Them Value for Having a Relationship With You

I love what Tatsuya Nakagawa wrote when asked about 15 quick ways to create value.[12] His first response was creating and forwarding relevant articles. This is true and something each 501(c) can do for free. The reason you exist is to help. The way you help is unique, and there are many around the nation and the globe who would benefit if you told them how.

We reflect value when we communicate the "how to" of our experience through stories of success and failure. It is as if we are putting a warm coat around the shoulders of the one reading our article. We make it about them, and when we share what is valuable to us, we create value for them.

Creating a Bridge

Our articles become a bridge connecting the next generation of donors to our organization. As a nonprofit, there are many valuable things we do for those who know us. The ability to become a producer of information can become the greatest long-term value provided by your organization. Many of us are consumers of information whether it is on Facebook or reading blogs or listening to podcasts. The digital marketing model that is so effective and ready to be adopted by nonprofits like yours is based upon the foundation of no longer being consumers but rather producers of high-value information.

What is the first step in transforming your nonprofit into a producer? In this next chapter, we will learn how to discover who our audience is.

WORKING IT OUT

Three Questions

Language Lesson #1: Who is my ideal donor?

_____

_____

_____

Language Lesson #2: Where online do they gather?

Type of stores they go to: _____

Social media connections: _____

Group chats: _____

Facebook groups: _____

Language Lesson #3: What portals are free and already available?

_____   _____

_____   _____

_____   _____

_____   _____

CHAPTER 4

MASTERING THE FUNDAMENTALS OF BUILDING ONLINE RELATIONSHIPS

"Build Relationships, Not Links."
—Scott Wyden Kivowitz

I was meeting with a group of nonprofit leaders in San Diego when one looked at me and asked, "How does a nonprofit escape the 'donor desert?'"

This is a great question that many of us have asked, and my answer is, "Each individual nonprofit organization must master the core principles of building relationships online."

"How do we do this?"

Let's take a look.

Have a Fresh Look at Yourself

I love the phrase *"Know oneself to know one's audience."* Your goal is not to get everyone to connect with you, but to know what it is about your organization that is "sticky" and discover the audience that wants to get stuck. Who are the people who will feel what you feel and want to see what you are seeing?

You may think you know what your nonprofit is. But do you? Do you have your core statistics readily at hand, and do you know your core story? It's kind of like the statistical research behind a well-designed business plan. Who are you? What are you accomplishing? How are you meeting the need? What can you improve on? When is the best time to act in a certain direction? Where are you going in the next four years, and, more importantly, what are the core statistics for your field of expertise as a nonprofit over the past four years?

Let's look at your core statistics.

- How much income have you achieved, and where did it come from?
  - Grants
  - Private donors
  - Fundraisers
  - Online Fundraising
  - Earned Income

Now project those numbers one to four years out and graph them.

- What are the national statistics and local statistics for nonprofits with your focus?
- How effective have your programs been? Use numbers and data, not critiques and compliments from people who like you. Graph the numbers.
- Who is best served by your nonprofit?
- What are the six-month outcomes from successes?
- Where does your nonprofit have the greatest impact?
- How do you know what you know, and what's the plan to upskill?
- When is the best time in the annual calendar to connect with potential donors for the "big ask"? Use national statistics, not just your experience. Be as specific as possible.

You will most likely think of even more questions to research.

Now that you have the statistics to base a very real assessment on who you are, you can speak factually and confidently about where you're going and what your challenges or "pain points" are going to be. This creates strategy markers for your team and organization.

Are you ready to name your niche? What is the specific place you hold in the nonprofit marketplace? Do you have a direct point of impact? You need to be able to say "yes" to each of these questions.

You might now want to jump to the next step and say, "I can write my core story and the big 'why' we are needed!" But you are not ready yet. You need to go through the process of understanding your audience before your write your core story.

I appreciate Benyamin Elias's 2021 article "'Know Your Audience' is a Lie, But it Still Matters,"[13] written for an email and CRM program we like called Active Campaign. In the article, he clearly describes the six criteria to look at to "know your audience," or KYA. I have read and heard many fundraisers communicate on this subject, and Benyamin does it better than most. So, I'm borrowing a number of the following thoughts from him.

Understand Your Audience

It is important to understand your audience, but it is unrealistic to truly know them. Many marketers may promise this superpower, but in truth, your ability to thoroughly know your audience is unrealistic unless you spend a lifetime with them. This is outside the realm of possibility.

It is better to say that we want to understand them as best as possible and then tailor our communication to them in the best way for a connection. Then we will try it again with a different style and observe the response to see if it was better.

To do this, first, we take one type of communication and categorize it "test sample A." Then we take a second differing communication and label it "B." After we run them both, we can compare their responses. In this way, we are constantly A/B testing or "split testing" our communication and learning how to relate more precisely to our desired audience.

We do this with our loved ones. When I first saw Michelle, she caught me "checking her out." What was I doing? Well, I was trying to figure out how to approach her. Once I got the nerve to make first contact, I realized my approach needed improving so I ran through several simulations in my head and with my friends, and then I approached her again. It went better this time, and we became friends. We built a relationship that has now lasted years and produced kiddos. Building relationships for a nonprofit is much the same but uses a "batch" method instead of one-on-one.

What is a "batch" method? It would be exhausting to connect with hundreds or thousands of people one-on-one. This is why we use apps, social platforms, and programs that will do the connecting for us. Why is it that an Instagram or TikTok influencer can have 7 million followers and hundreds of thousands of fans who think they are best friends with the online powerhouse?

It is simply the skill of knowing their niche and consistently packaging communication in a format that speaks to the heart of their followers. It's mass relationship building by speaking to one specific interest in a way that produces feelings and emotional responses. They communicate in a way that makes their reader or viewer feel hope or a sense of empowerment. They encourage their followers to escape their present for a moment and arrive at a new idea.

The influencer becomes skilled at introducing the fan to an increased place of "status" because of association. This is why people who follow Joe Rogan are quick to say, "When I was listening to Rogan the other day…" Their association with him makes them feel like their status is greater.

The skilled influencers are also able to simply cause the individual to feel one of the "big three" market drivers (relationship, health, or wealth) because they read the email or watched the post or listened to the podcast.

It's important to understand that relationships are the same all over the world. You need to spend time to understand the one you want to connect with, or you will come off as cheap and salesy no matter how pure your intent.

This concept is also true for a nonprofit. Take a look at the following website for a rehab clinic written by copywriter Joanna Wiebe:

Before Joanna started working on this website's home page, the clinic was only focused on the problem. They were trying to connect to addicts by putting up descriptions and pictures accentuating their problems. The clinic didn't consider that the ones viewing the site were most likely to be the loved ones looking for a solution for their family member or friend. The clinic, with Joanna's help, now began searching for wording that would instead connect to the pain felt by the most probable viewers, the family members or friends.

Because this vitally important and busy rehab clinic took the time to research and know its audience, the clinic was able to start to understand the probabilities of the most likely online search criteria that would drive those in need to their offered solution. Additionally, they gave the wording (or copy) "Break free of the grip of substance abuse and addiction today" a tone of hope and success, truly connecting to the emotional driver of the viewers.

As a result, their digital marketing content improved. Their new messaging grew by over 400% in button clicks alone. Their form submissions increased by 20%, and their ability to connect to the local community increased dramatically.

The Big Six Graphs

You can find a lot of bad audience research advice trolling for you all over the internet. It's important to understand the grid *you* should use to identify who your audience is. Here are the six ways to graph your audience statistics:

1. Demographics
2. Analytics
3. Psychographics
4. Review Mining
5. Online Chats
6. Interviews with Real People.

Let's Talk Demographics

When we launch a new nonprofit, the first thing we do is create a demographic study. This is the study of populations, as in their education, nationality, religion, and ethnicity. You will find even greater detail as you dive into population studies that compare the relationships between economic, social, cultural, and biological processes influencing a population. The Merriam-Webster dictionary[14] dives into even greater detail, describing "demographics" as "the study of a population especially with regard to density and capacity for expansion or decline."

But demographics get complicated quickly. When you start researching statistical study populations, you need to consider these factors:

- Accurately sampling large populations
- Population size
- Population dynamics
- Sampling bias
- Direct vs. indirect ways of gathering data

When you are using demographics to create a donor profile, it's also important to understand another caveat. The demographic profile you think will benefit most from your organization's activity isn't necessarily the same profile as the person who will donate to your nonprofit.

There's a definite difference between talking to a mature family, where the adults are in their 40s, and a single person in their 20s. One may be perfect for volunteering; another will be great as a potential donor. Which one would your service benefit, and which one will empathize with the need and donate monthly because of the value you bring?

Though this information is important, the difficulty is that it does not tell you how your audience feels. Sometimes we get lost in having too much information from the demographic research. As a result, we get tricked into drilling down on the wrong group of statistics.

Let's understand our demographics and use them for a quick filter through our best potential donors. If you say, "We impact families dealing with drug addiction," then everyone else who does not empathize or relate will leave you alone. This is exactly what you're aiming for.

What's crucial is that you don't stop at demographics. You need more information to create well targeted marketing messages.

Understanding Online Analytics

Everywhere I look in the digital marketing space, I see the catchphrase "data-driven" marketing. Free platforms like Google Analytics have created an ease and accessibility to statistics concerning interest in your website and funnels. This makes it easy to track the effectiveness of using a digital approach for finding donors and creating revenue.

I love using Facebook PPC Ads (Pay Per Click) because the analytics are immediate, and I can quickly adjust the wording and focus of a nonprofit paid driver (ad) campaign. This allows me to easily see my ROI (Return on Investment) used on the platform.

This also allows me to send the message to the right people at the right time. When does my audience open their Facebook page? Or at what time of the day and day of the week are they most likely to pull out their wallet and use a credit card? Analytics will show me.

As an example of the A/B or "split" testing we talked about at the beginning of the chapter, a nonprofit can send two different messages to solicit the same response to two different groups of 100 people and watch the analytics to see which one tracks better. Then, you take the most effective one and use it for the next week to drive viewers to your email-attraction or donation funnel.

You can create competing funding events on your website and advertise them both over a seven-day period to see which ones cause specific visitors to act.

Your results from taking the time to A/B test then will allow you to retarget people who showed interest in your funnel or website but moved on.

Now you can try a different approach to solicit their buy-in to your mission.

By seeing where your visitors click next on your site, a nonprofit can strategize what will transition them from "looky-loos" into your next long-term donors.

Exploring Psychographics

Simply defined, psychographics is the research of the psychology of an audience or donor group.

Organizations enjoy a significant leap forward when they start using psychographics because it tells them what their donors genuinely care about.

For example, when we take John Smith's demographic information, we may discover these facts about him:

- He is in his mid-40s.
- His income is $85,000/yr.
- He manages a youth Little League.
- He oversees the marketing department at the local car dealership.

However, a psychographic study will point out even more:

- He battles to balance his job responsibilities and Little League.
- He wants to start vlogging on social media sites.
- He is wanting to move into a more lucrative career but doesn't know how to negotiate the transition.
- His hobby is kayaking, which takes up a lot of his extra time.

This cache of data will point you to the online networks that will attract John's attention to your nonprofit. The power of advertising directly on kayaking forums and job transition support groups would allow you to connect with many people like John.

This is your target donor group.

Psychographic data also communicates how wide your reach can be. The Activities, Interests, and Opinions (AIO) variables used by this kind of research are especially valuable.

Imagine a profile of a core part of the population within the city where your nonprofit is based. We can then boil down this descriptive to a woman called Maggie. We know that Maggie loves to go on dates on Friday night and play sports like softball or soccer. These are her Activities.

We also have learned by the algorithm following her online photograph postings and reposts she has shared on her Instagram account that she loves the outdoors, is concerned about the warming of the planet, and loves kittens. These are her Interests.

Finally, our data provided by Facebook noted that she is liking a lot of Black Lives Matter news articles. Her time spent on articles concerning indigenous justice issues is longer than her other viewings, and she has unfriended a number of Trump supporters. As a result, we can assume Maggie is most likely progressive in ideology. These are her Opinions.

Now you are able to be more concentrated on your donor connection and better comprehend your donors' motivations.

To connect with the Maggies in your community, it may be helpful to have pictures of outdoor activities that will cause the person scrolling on their mobile device to pause for a split second. Then their eye sees the kitten in the background of your picture or video, and the viewer smiles and pauses a second more. You decide to not use the wording "Make your neighborhood great again" but rather "Click here to bring change to your neighborhood." They CLICK...

However, in creating your specific message, you will need something else, and that is the perfect wording for the message you want to convey. Hang with me just a little bit more, and I will cover exactly what you need to say.

We call this the skill of copywriting, and you would be writing the copy. Using the right words so you engage your potential donor is a skill all in itself. One of America's most renowned copywriters, Gary Bencivenga, said this:

> "The vast majority of products are sold because of the need for love, the fear of shame, the pride of achievement, the drive for recognition, the yearning to feel important, the urge to look attractive, the lust for power, the longing for romance, the need to feel secure, the terror of facing the unknown, the lifelong hunger for self-esteem, and so on.

"Emotions are the fire of human motivation, the combustible force that secretly drives most decisions to buy. When your marketing harnesses those forces correctly you will generate explosive increases in response."[15]

So, let's talk about how you can create messages that elicit strong emotions that drive people to action.

British advertising legend David Ogilvy insisted that the team around him communicate in the common exchange used every day. He said:

"Unless you have some reason to be solemn and pretentious, write your copy in the colloquial language which your customers use in everyday conversation."[16]

How do your donors talk? What slang do they use? At what education level do they like to read? The best words you can use in your copy are found in the mouths of your donors.

Are you listening to them when they are speaking to you? Are they even speaking to you at all? In the previous chapter, we looked at where you go to surround yourself with the target group that your statistics and psychographics point out are the best possible donor group.

Compelling messages use the exact words your audience uses to describe their own problems. That's why knowing your audience is so important. And all you need to do is get your audience to tell you about their problems in their own words.

Following are three tactics you can use to get the exact words your audience uses.

Review Mining

"If you think you need rehab, you do!"

Remember that headline? I mentioned it earlier, but here it is again.

Joanna Wiebe is a great copywriter, but this headline was not written by her. She plucked it out of someone else's mouth.

This is called review mining.

The original headline on this website was an overused and tired opening which said, "Your Addiction Ends Here." I have often seen headlines like that on marketing websites.

But where do you think the new headline came from? Joanna was researching and came across an Amazon review on a book that focused on ending addiction.

Seriously?

Online reviews are a huge database of language that is used by your donors and your community. When people leave comments and reviews, they will communicate both positive and negative language that is invaluable to you.

- You will hear their pain points.
- You will discover what they love from their own vocabulary.
- They share how an organization or product helped them.
- They expand on what they wish could be done or how a group could have done better.

This sounds like gold, doesn't it? If you are a nonprofit involved in the musical arts, you can try out review mining using Amazon reviews. Look at books on the arts and read reviews on publications that speak directly about nonprofit performing arts centers or nonprofit dance groups and studios. Insert your group and change your search, and you will find many reviews about your niche within the nonprofit world.

It will help you find better messages. And it's something you can do right now.

Online Chats

Amazon reviews are not the only place your future donors are gathering and chatting. Facebook, Twitter, Reddit, Quora, and chat forums are only a few of the many places where they are gathering.

I would encourage you to take 15 minutes and write down all the online networking groups that may be housing your next monthly donor. If you are a music and dance nonprofit, you could go on Twitch for free and follow the amazing musicians there. Just listen to their great conversations.

If you are an outdoors group that focuses on fitness, you could join online chat groups and networking sites that are discussing the greatest hikes or camping spots in your area. A job prep nonprofit should not have to look hard to discover conversations between HR managers and business owners, job placement advice chat rooms, and recruitment professionals high fiving each other. I think you get the idea.

The big takeaway is that you get to see and understand how your potential donors are feeling and viewing life.

Interviews with Real People

Review mining and online conversations are an attractive place to start because they can be done literally right now.

Open Google, type in "[your nonprofit category] reviews," and you'll get messaging ideas immediately.

But at the same time, you cannot deny the power and clarity you can receive from real, live interviews with real, live people.

When I started the process of writing this book, I reached out to nonprofit leaders on LinkedIn and Facebook and asked if I could chat with them about the focus of this book. The conversations were direct and full of useful information that altered the flow and subjects we were considering.

One of the biggest struggles with being limited to online conversations is having less availability for a follow-up question. One of my favorites is simply, "Tell me more." You will find yourself asking it over and over, and you will discover very compelling messages hiding in your future donor's head.

That's impossible on a Reddit thread that closed three years ago.

Actual face-to-face (or phone-to-phone) conversations are hands-down the best way to know your audience, and as a result, you will be able to create better copy.

A donor interview gives you the opportunity to ask questions like these:

- What's the hardest part about _____?
- How does _____ make you feel?
- When you connected with a _____ charity, what were you thinking about?
- Where do you go to find information about _____?
- How well does _____ solve your problem?

And then you say, "Tell me more." You get to hear real, personal stories, ones that lead to great copy and marketing messages.

Now You Can Write Your Core Story

Understanding your future donors is also understanding the need for your organization to grow and to make growth a priority. This is not something you can do in a conference room. You need to talk to real people.

The wonderful thing about this process is that it allows you to uncover the deep, burning pain points of your donors and the language they use to describe those pain points. Then you can confidently script brilliantly accurate marketing messages.

The first three things we spoke about, demographics, psychographics, and analytics, convert the behavioral data so you can see how the people visiting your funnel page and website are acting. Review mining, online chat rooms, and interviews allow you to discover how they are feeling. Your research will allow you to convert the right words into powerful copy and see the results of your messaging skills.

Now you can write your core story, who you are and what drives your passion within your niche. Once this is done, you face a larger question: Who's going to read it? Let's dive into that next.

WORKING IT OUT

Three Questions

What are the best available dates to conduct or order a demographics and psychographics study for my nonprofit?

    A. Demographics   _____/_____/_____

    B. Psychographics   _____/_____/_____

Where are 12 online sites to do review mining focused on my specific nonprofit niche?

   1. _____   2. _____   3. _____

   4. _____   5. _____   6. _____

   7. _____   8. _____   9. _____

   10. _____   11. _____   12. _____

Whom should I delegate to set up the phone or Zoom interviews with real people, and what questions should they ask? Delegated to: _____

_____

    Question #1: _____

    Question #2: _____

    Question #3: _____

    Question #4: _____

    Question #5: _____

REACHING DONORS FROM ACROSS THE NATION AND AROUND THE WORLD

"If you think you are the entire picture, you will never see the big picture."
—John Maxwell

We moved from New Zealand to the United States because my father was asked to become dean of a school for nonprofit leaders and founders. At the age of 8, I found myself in Ridgecrest, CA, population 25,000.

It was definitely small-town life. Each hot summer day when my mother took us to Thrifty's Drug Store to get a 25-cent ice cream cone, we would run into people we knew. It was our social moment of the week. Then I would get on my BMX bike and ride all the way across to the other side of town to play at my friend's house. It took all of 20 minutes.

This is the same as living in a small or mid-sized nonprofit. We know everyone, and all our systems are memorized. We go from day to day, hoping we see someone we know when we go to Starbucks so we can have *our* "social moment" of the week.

The problem is, we start to become insular in our thinking and our understanding of how to project ourselves, and our influence becomes smaller and smaller.

Gabriel is a talented trustee on the board of a nonprofit I started working with in 2020. The first time I met him, we were talking about building email-attraction and donation funnels, and he asked a question I am often asked: "Why would someone from across the United States care about our nonprofit, and why would they want to support us?"

What a great question to ask, and before sharing my response with you, it is probably best to point out this is the core description of a micro-community. When we see what we do as important in our town or city but do not realize how important the lessons and experiences can be beyond our current borders, we are living and thinking inside our micro-community.

The true answer to Gabriel's question is, "You are right. No one beyond the local people who benefit from your care and service cares about your existence." There are no pain points people outside the current connections have to drive them toward Gabriel's mission. His nonprofit did not offer the unknown donor any possible value.

The core principle of the email-attraction funnel and the several different styles of donation funnels is to create a bridge between the nonprofit and the new possible donor. They need to feel your pain and find relief from their own pain through information produced by you.

Signs that You are Stuck

What are some of the ways you may know your nonprofit is stuck in a micro-community? Let's call it a "mi-com."

1. You know exactly who all your donors are. You may also know who their kids are and what their dogs' names are. If it's Friday night, you can be almost certain of the bar they'll be at, the shots they'll be doing, and the songs they're losing their minds over. You might be in a mi-com.
2. Your office is a swinging donor door. They come in and out, asking questions, giving suggestions and anecdotes you didn't ask for. If

they start telling you a story of a person who is needing to do such-and-such and correct so-and-so, you realize they're talking about you. You might be in a mi-com.

3. Donors call you to talk about their personal life. You are their favorite person to discuss vacation plans and doctor visits. It's like the one-horse setup in the middle of Iowa where, if you want to do anything besides chill in a cornfield and hang out with your cousin, you're going to have to change. You might be in a mi-com.

4. You find yourself looking at other nonprofit fundraisers the way some people look at the dream boat, car, or vacation. If entire folders on your computer are dedicated to well-designed fundraisers, amazing stories of donors, and panoramic displays of nonprofit conferences you hope one day to go to, you might be in a mi-com.

5. If you are embarrassed by your donors and your nonprofit, and you pause when someone asks you where you work, you might be in a mi-com.

You may be giving up on your dreams simply because of the constant limitations of fewer and fewer donors. There are dreams we all have, dreams that started when we began the journey along the nonprofit path. They mature with us until they become a persistent thought. I remember times when I would imagine what my life would be like if I only had the courage to chase after it. With the limits our current vision for new donors places on us, the frustrations start to come to the surface. We move in baby steps closer to the edge, because down deep inside, we know there is a larger donor base available, if only we could find a way to access it.

Six Signs You're Expanding Into a Macro-Community

As you begin to realize you are only a funnel away from breaking into a national or worldwide community, there are a few things you should be prepared for.

1. You discover who your true donors are. This may shock you, but when you are raising funding from sources outside your community,

sometimes there is a struggle with your local donors. It isn't unusual for a donor within the micro-community to feel jealous or threatened when your survival is not determined by their support. However, those donors who genuinely love what you're doing will be excited for you and will run even faster alongside you.

2. Your perception changes. When you are in a tight-knit community, issues often become one-sided and personal. When you are producing articles for your expanded audience, your view of your immediate surroundings changes. Your perspective becomes more global, and the sense of strength and opportunity can be exciting and create fresh waves of hope.

3. When you reach beyond your micro-community, you can become a curiosity and a mystery to the locals. They become curious about this new breath of creativity and stories of impact beyond their comfortable mental walls. An appropriate, well-known quote here is, "The less you reveal, the more people can wonder." You should feed the excitement and let the local donors know of the victories you are having in the macro-community, but don't overcommunicate. Keep some mystery for yourself.

4. In the macro-community, you are suddenly a nobody, and it feels great. You get to redefine your self-identity. You get to re-engage the world without leaving your base. By the time I was 23, I was married to Michelle, and we were traveling to India to work with a group of youth-focused nonprofits. We were still heavily involved with our nonprofits at home but stepping beyond those walls changed us. When we came home, the "bigness" of our experience came home with us. We saw immediate positive impact. It's the same when your writing starts to impact lives from New York to British Columbia. It will change you, and you can bring that largeness back into your local nonprofit.

5. You appreciate your local nonprofit more. Not only have you shared its ability to create value to a larger audience, but you have also been instrumental in its transformation. That is always exciting.

6. Finally, you discover who you are. You start to find yourself. It allows you to expand and learn more about what makes you tick, and your horizons become boundless.

What you have is an ability to impact lives. You can become the catalyst that reduces the frustration and pain. It's not a bad trade, and at the end of the exchange, your nonprofit gets what it needs as well: a new connection to a future donor.

Once you've committed to move from the small pond of donors into the large lake, and from the lake into the ocean, what's the next step? It's the creation of a unique and powerful nonprofit value ladder.

WORKING IT OUT

Three Questions

Re-drawing Your Borders:

What are the borders of our nonprofit's current influence?

Geographically: _____

Human Connections: _____

Social Online: _____

Email: _____

Where can they be 12 months from now?

Geographically: _____

Human Connections: _____

Social Online: _____

Email: _____

Where do I want them to be?

Geographically: _____

Human Connections: _____

Social Online: _____

Email: _____

CHAPTER 6

WRITING TO WIN HEARTS AND BUILD LONG-TERM DONORS

"Start with your offer, tell a story to increase its value, then discover your hook."
—Russell Brunson -
Dotcom Secrets

So, the big challenge is, can you connect with a person in one sentence? Then, can you communicate effectively in a way that draws them to the decision you want them to arrive at? Finally, do you challenge them in a way that compels action?

Russell Brunson says it well when he writes about the three steps of Hook, Story, and Offer and defines each step in detail in his *Dotcom Secrets* trilogy. The difficulty arrives because when we speak of commerce, ROI, and increasing income, our nonprofit community likes to use a different vocabulary. Though the end result and meanings can often be the same, many nonprofits don't like to communicate using the economic marketplace wording. It's true that there are some regulations we must consider, and we are responsible stewards of the income produced for community purposes. But the exchange of values for revenue is still the fulcrum point that 501(c)s and incorporated businesses must equally understand to succeed.

As Brunson suggests, we should start at the end of our report and understand what our fixed outcome should be. We are not selling a product, though, and therefore do not have an offer. We are, instead, challenging a donor. What is our target for our report or article? Where do we want to lead them at the conclusion? Certainly, we want to provoke an action, but the degree of action is based solely on the stage within the value ladder we are strategizing the use of the article for.

My childhood friend, Ron, is the owner of a native fashion brand. He runs an e-commerce business that champions products created by Indigenous populations and promotes the products back to the native peoples. Because of his background, the subject of colonial appropriation has come up many times and is a concern to Ron and his family.

Ron is also an amazing poet and is adept at putting words together. On several occasions he has helped me with large-scale productions we have collaborated on over the years. Before he goes onstage and performs a powerful recitation of poetry, with the drums beating, guitars grinding, and keyboard adding atmosphere, he is writing. He begins writing each presentation by asking one question: "What is the one point of the performance?"

Whether he is communicating about justice inequality for Indigenous peoples, or speaking poetry to captivated audiences, he always starts by needing to know where the words are going. When we're building a report to launch a donor funnel or a funding campaign, the same is true for you and me.

A Challenge that Creates Action

To start your creative process at the conclusion or end is where the great challenge lies. For Ron, he may be wanting to end his poem inspiring the listener to voice their unity for missing and murdered Indigenous women. This is a shocking human rights crisis that disproportionately affects Indigenous peoples in Canada and the United States, notably those in the First Nations, Metis, Inuit (Canadian education), and Native American communities. It is heartbreaking and desperately needs to be addressed.

Either by poetry, speaking, and or in writing, Ron's final challenge is where he begins. A challenge to stand, a challenge to overcome fear, a challenge to not let hope die. What is your challenge? What is the single driving point about your nonprofit that wakes you up early and keeps you excited throughout the day? How do we enlarge it and make it a value point to bring the reader to a decision for action?

Here are some ideas:

Food Pantry – "Prepare for winter shortages by stocking these five foods before November."

Dance Group – "Do these three exercises to keep yourself limber at any age."

Medical Care for Autism – "Download this free report to identify the stages of Asperger's, what it means, and whom you should call."

Justice Policy Nonprofit – "Forward this link to a friend and email us your story."

Professional Placement Organization– "Download this script for your resume, fill it out today, and send it to us for a 100% free review."

I think you get the idea.

Communicating in Word Pictures

My adopted uncle and late father's best friend is Tony Anthony. Tony was born in the streets of India, a part of the lowest caste system: an "untouchable." He had a brilliant mind, and before the age of 13, he started to teach himself. Soon, as a young teenager, he was speaking publicly in several languages. He began to not only see himself lifted out of poverty, but also to lift out many of the other "untouchables" around him.

For decades, Tony Anthony has personally impacted millions of people in many countries. Through his direct leadership, churches have been built and thousands of jobs have been created. Tony has been the driver behind many schools which have been launched that are open to any religion, and homes and orphanages that are being built wherever his teams travel. He designed them to run independently and connect as a network through relationships and communication, not a formal corporate organization, and he teaches them everything he knows so success can follow them.

The brilliant thing about Tony and why you can't stop listening to him and cheering him on boils down to this: He is skilled at communicating in stories. He builds verbal pictures that allow you to see exactly where he is, and you start to believe you are right there with him. Whether it's a biblical passage where you clearly imagine the dusty street and the palm frond in your hand, or the story of a village with flies swarming around the food you're trying to put in your mouth, his word pictures are perfect.

As you communicate your stories, use the adjectives and adverbs that color in the stories and communicate the emotion within. Let the reader feel, see, and understand the journey taking place.

Intellectual Writing vs. Empathic Writing

There are generally two types of people who are trying to communicate: the intellectuals and the empaths. When writing a grant or going before a board, we need to keep in mind that the statistics and legal argument needed to persuade a decision on our behalf is determined on an intellectual argument. Statistics are important, and ramifications must be highlighted, but these are not always the communications we need at a particular time. I find the following Funding Cave chart helpful:

Empaths (Create Connection)	Intellectuals (Declare Facts)
Donor Communication	Grant Application
Emotional	Legal
Story	Statistics
Build Relationship	Get Approval

Now that we have a clear understanding of the end result and the stories that will draw the heart into the challenge, it's time to build your connection to the donor.

Your Connect Needs to Hook the Donor

The Golden Rule of connecting to your new donors is to lead with honesty, integrity, understanding, empathy, and thoughtfulness. The Connect has to grab the donors' attention, but also has to be real. Here is a split test you can look at to see the distinction:

Alarming	vs.	**A call to action**
Thousands Will Die		*Know the Steps to Survive*
This Winter!		*the Winter!*
Sensational	vs.	**Purposeful**
Your Kids Have Autism!		*The Autism Test,*
		So You Know.
Fear-inducing	vs.	**Hopeful**
Is Your Child in a Gang?		*Relationships That Keep*
		Your Kids Gang Free.
Demanding	vs.	**Directing**
Are You a Racist?		*Understanding What*
Decide Now!		*"Black Lives Matter" Means.*
Demeaning	vs.	**Encouraging**
You're an Idiot		*How to Make Informed*
If You Eat Meat.		*Food Choices.*
Disrespectful	vs.	**Honorable**
10 Things that Prove		*How to Know You Have*
Your Man's a Pig.		*a High-Class Man.*

Let's use the examples given in the challenge to see how the flow works from title and connect, to communication, to ending with a clear challenge.

For a Food Pantry

Title: "By November, Make Sure These Five Foods Are In Your Pantry!"

Connect: "Over the last decade, we have seen a need for these five items…"

Story: Suzy last winter - **Point**: it got her through.

Story: Last winter, José and his family - **Point**: We supplied the five.

Story: Margaret and her two kids - **Point**: She has them already and is confident.

Challenge: Encourage the reader to prepare for winter shortages by stocking these five foods before November. Contact us with any questions.

Now it's your turn to try. Write out on a whiteboard or open a Google Doc and start. What is the challenge? Do a basic frame of three stories you can fill in later. Create the connect and give yourself a title. Boom! You've got it. Great job.

Yes, you have a voice, and it has value. Now, what about your nonprofit's value in the community, and how does that form your funnel campaign's values ladder? Let's look at this in the next two chapters.

WORKING IT OUT

Three Questions

For each subject, can you write a <u>Connect</u>?

    1. Diabetes statistics   Hook: _____

    2. Morning exercise   Hook: _____

    3. Baby crying at night   Hook: _____

    4. Fish tank care   Hook: _____

    5. Outdoor ideas   Hook: _____

    6. Singing voice care   Hook: _____

    7. Suicide hotline   Hook: _____

    8. Racial justice   Hook: _____

What stories "<u>Communicate the success</u>" of your nonprofit?

(Hint: Make it about a specific person or animal, not a statistic.)

Name: _____ Point: _____

Name: _____ Point: _____

Name: _____ Point: _____

Can you write a <u>Challenge</u>, a call to action, for each of your above points?

Call to Action: _____

Call to Action: _____

Call to Action: _____

*Feel free to post any of your answers on our Facebook group chat for encouraging responses and constructive input.

CHAPTER 7

REALIZING GLOBAL VALUE INSIDE YOUR NONPROFIT

"Your value ladder becomes the brick-by-brick road of solutions that are designed to get you to your 'OZ.'"
—Stacey and Paul Martino

M aria was sitting in the bedroom going through her emails when something caught her eye.

"Juan, come in here and look at this."

"What is it, honey?" Juan mumbles as he walks into the bedroom to look over her shoulder.

She pointed to the laptop screen and an open email. It was an invitation for their family to audition for a whole season of free beginner music and dance lessons in the neighborhood.

"I bet there's a catch," Juan said as he turned and walked out of the room.

"Well, I'm going to drop by the place tomorrow and see. I'll let you know," Maria shouted at his back as he disappeared out the bedroom door and down the hallway.

This is how nearly 200 families connected with the San Diego Performing

Arts Center every quarter. My colleague, Janelle, helped me design a relationship ladder which started with the connection to the neighborhood and built it up until it ended with core families donating time and resources to the programs of the Center.

What is a Value Ladder?

A nonprofit value ladder is an ascending set of offers that increase in commitment and value and connect with people where they are in their journey to becoming a core participant—from initial recognition to their final decision to support the nonprofit's purpose physically or financially. A value ladder is an effective way for a nonprofit to build trust and maximize a lifetime relationship with each donor.

Basically, you start by offering something of value for free and then increase the commitment to connect with each new step in the journey.

Basic psychology has proven that connecting with any new relationship, especially a donor, is predicated on a sense of safety. If someone comes to you and says, "This is why you need to give me money," you would be, at the least, put off and, at most, horrified. The long-term chance for a relationship is nearly nil.

In truth, all nonprofits need to build a relationship with potential donors to ensure attaining our goals and assuring the success of our missions.

How do we honestly connect with others in a way that does not put them off?

We need/want the future donors to feel happy they connected with us and thankful we exist in their lives. Even more, they are asking to be a part of our organization. The reason this happens is because we are offering a value much higher than the ask, and more importantly, we do not ask until the value is felt.

The Performing Arts Center used its value ladder skillfully to attract and keep its donors. Many may call it a branding strategy, but I would rather say it's a service or connection strategy. You brand your nonprofit to create a look and feel that reflects your niche and service. Your value ladder folds into your branding package in look, color, font, and feel, but the purpose for each step can be altered. It is guiding the donors' journey and your connection to them along the way. The road to each charity is unique, but the donors' journey to decide whether or not to like you is similar.

The Donor Discovery Journey

A value ladder takes potential donors by the hand from the very first connection and walks side by side with them as they grow to trust you. We call this the **Donor Discovery Journey**.

The Donor Discovery Journey looks something like this:

Awareness → Free value exchange for email address. No trust level yet and your nonprofit donor doesn't want to feel pain, only wants to be relieved of pain.

Testing → Connecting story w/added value for a small donation. Now the donor is considering trusting you. They still do not want to feel any pain and they want to be reassured of their possible decision to support you.

Deliberation → This is where you as a nonprofit need to be a bit more vulnerable. The donor wants to feel like they have been privy to a direct introduction and have also received more added value for a larger donation. The donor has begun to journey into limited trust of you and your organization. They still do not want to feel any pain and wants to know your pain or "points of struggle" are managed.

Conclusion → This is where you need a strong connection event with core commitment equal to value received. Now your donor trusts your organization and feels that being associated with you is an increase of status within their social peers. They start to become willing to help you with your pain points and are willing to absorb a limited increase of their own discomfort or pain points.

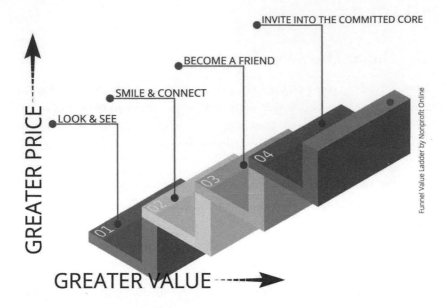

INVITE INTO THE COMMITTED CORE

BECOME A FRIEND

SMILE & CONNECT

LOOK & SEE

GREATER PRICE

GREATER VALUE ---->

Funnel Value Ladder by Nonprofit Online

Creating a Value Statement for Your Nonprofit

The first step is creating a value statement. This is simple and goes like this:

We help (whom) to (result) through (opportunity).
Who is the person you want to serve?
What is the result you want provide?
What is the new opportunity you want to offer?

Organization's Value Ladder

Jim and Sandy were standing at the gravesite of their son Joshua. Following the recent collapse of the Berlin Wall, they had come to the Ukraine from California to help in the aftermath. Their son Joshua was born a few months after they arrived, but because of a medical mistake he never left the hospital. Jim and Sandy's cost of caring came at the ultimate price, and their devastation was complete.

In the season that followed, their emotional pain was intense, and though they were encouraged to come home, they chose to stay and continue helping. As their emotional fog started to lift, they began seeing the streets in their Ukrainian city through different eyes.

They began to ask about the young children hiding in the shadows and eating in the alleys. The stories they heard horrified them. There were huge criminal rings trafficking children from the farms and streets of the city to the ports of Turkey. The few children who escaped ended up hiding among the street garbage cans where they would scavenge food and clothing. Jim and Sandy found their purpose. They were able to raise enough support to open the first safe place named after their son: "Joshua House." They had created a safe home for their new children.

The effort to build more Joshua Houses was enormous, and funding was central to their success. They chose to begin their relationship with potential new donors by creating a free monthly newsletter that, to this day, is still sent regularly. It not only tells amazing and heroic stories of these children but also encourages hope for the reader.

The newsletter allowed people to become emotionally invested before anything was asked of them. Soon, television shows wanted to interview them. From this exposure, donors began to connect. Extra value was added by acknowledging these followers and emailing them updates.

Next, Jim and Sandy visited the U.S. with a number of the children they had rescued. They wanted to give them the opportunity to experience a bigger world. The children visited pockets of donors where smiles and stories were exchanged and created stronger relationships.

They followed with an invitation to come help serve at the children's summer camp to physically connect many donors to the success at Joshua House. Jim and Sandy gave love, hope, and kindness to all who connected to them, whether or not they donated. The money was not the goal. Sharing the improvement in the lives of these children was, and the donations followed. As an invested donor, you would feel proud to stand with them and excited for every new child that was freed and given hope and a chance for a peaceful life.

Did you see their value ladder? Do you catch how it progressed? Though the focus is never the money, money is necessary, and donors follow in the increased velocity of the value given to them. Their value ladder started with the newsletter (encouraging and full of stories) and ended with the donor physically helping and connecting to them in their efforts.

Jim and Sandy's value statement could say this:

Joshua House helps <u>orphaned and abandoned children</u> to <u>heal, grow, and thrive</u> through <u>creating family, imparting faith, providing education, and birthing hope</u>.

The Joshua House Value Ladder is this:

Step 1: FREE Value Provide an encouraging newsletter.

Step 2: Small Time/Financial Investment + Added FREE Value Connect with emails imparting encouragement and opening the door for donation opportunities.

Step 3: Committed Donor + Increased Value Host Jim and the family as they speak to your organization and begin to build a genuine, healthy relationship. This creates strong, consistent support.

Step 4: High-Valued and Invested Supporter (Must have = Value) Come and volunteer for a short season, serving and helping at one of the homes. Create a lifetime connection where the individual will help directly carry the burden and be able to empathize with the core values of the nonprofit.

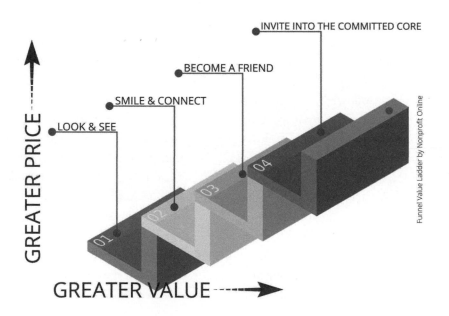

WORKING IT OUT

Three Questions

Let's build your nonprofit value ladder and connect to your community.

Step 1: What can we provide for free to our community?

- _____
- _____
- _____
- _____

Step 2: What can we provide inexpensively, and what free item can we attach?

- Item: _____
- Free add-on: _____
- Item: _____
- Free add-on: _____

Step 3: What can we provide at full price, and what free item can we attach?

- Item: _____
- Free add-on: _____
- Item: _____
- Free add-on: _____

CHAPTER 8

DESIGNING A HIGH-VALUE, ONLINE FUNNEL CAMPAIGN

"Strive not to be a success, but rather to be of value."
—Albert Einstein

Now that your nonprofit has its value ladder built, it's time to build a value ladder for your new email-attraction campaign and your donation funnels.

"Having your hand out to just keep the doors open is humiliating," Keith said to me when I asked him what the most difficult thing about fundraising was. The great thing about funnels is that you are doing exactly the opposite by creating an "irresistible offer" that will benefit the potential donor.

We often feel that a business's first imperative seems to be profit, but in reality it is to find and retain customers. How do they do this? By creating an "irresistible offer" that gives value to the shopper. In doing so, the business hopes to build a relationship with the customer.

A nonprofit organization's purpose is to meet a need, but the funding necessity requires it to find and retain donors. Money is a tool; it is neither good nor bad.

If you are a nonprofit founder, you are an entrepreneur at heart. Your success is predicated upon your ability to build upon a framework that is balanced between purpose and income. We want our purpose to be our battle flag, but we need our income to advance before our purpose. This is why it is important to avoid the "Seven Funding Nevers."

David Higgins' Seven Nonprofit Funding Nevers

1. **Never become desperate.** Build funnels before desperation sets in. When a nonprofit becomes desperate, it becomes foolish.
2. **Never hate your donors.** Build email-attraction funnels so you will always have more donors than the need. When you're frustrated with donors, it's because you don't have enough, and that's on you.
3. **Never become cocky.** Build funnels, seeing them as an answer to the income question and a sound business decision, not because, "They'll make us rich." Greed and cockiness go hand in hand, and donors hate them both.
4. **Never become highly emotional about funding.** Build donation funnels because it is the right thing to do. Highly emotional responses to funding cause us to be justified with high-risk decisions with funds. That never ends well.
5. **Never take on a fatalistic worldview**. Build funnels as an investment in longevity. Nonprofits were needed in the 1920s, are needed in the 2020s, and will still be needed in the 2120s. You will and you need to have a 10-year, 25-year, and 100-year plan for your nonprofits.
6. **Never stop investing in your future**. Build strong funnel strategies as an investment portfolio for your nonprofit. Historically, every five-to-seven years, the U.S. economy has a bear market that lasts for one and a half years. I have seen this consistently throughout my life. In every economic "bear market," donors disappear, and funding is choked. Without funnel funding to build up savings, a bear market is terrifying to nonprofits. If you are in the industry for another 30 years, you will be experiencing another three to four bear markets no matter how you vote.

7. **Never be unfocused.** Build funnels to support your passion. This is the time to emphasize what you love and fund your heart project. If you don't love your nonprofit direction, you will not be here for long. This is the time to change your fundraising activities, so you are excited to come to serve every morning.

Building Funnels

James spends all his available time rescuing amazing people caught in conflict areas around the globe through his organization, "These Numbers Have Faces." As incredibly skilled as he is at funding his nonprofit and guiding the people they help to restart their lives, the discovery of new donors and the reviving of the donor pipeline is his biggest challenge. He reports, "It can be so frustrating."

The beauty about well-designed email-attraction funnels is you don't need to look for donors; you just start communicating your bridge stories. These stories will connect curious people to your value ladder, and the donors will find you. They will download your interesting report or value article. When they take that action, it triggers the email campaign which automatically launches building a relationship with the potential donor. The email campaign introduces them to the donation funnel, and the small donations will start to come in. Do you see the progression?

Seven Funnels to Build Into an Online Strategy

Let's have a "1,000-foot view" of a funnel strategy that your nonprofit could use. If you take a funnel and lay it out like a map page by page, it will look like the following blueprints. In the digital marketing world, this is how we would draw out a funnel before building it. Let me introduce you to seven ideas for different funnels your nonprofit could use for connecting to your global community and to raise funding.

Blueprint 1: Our Recommended Email-Attraction Funnel

Purpose: Initial Connection

Action: Downloadable FREE Report

Email-attraction funnels are key to all long-term funding. Their power is the ability to acquire emails for a value item such as a relevant report or helpful article. This is a long-term funding solution because of the 1 email = $1 ratio in the industry per income cycle.

Some of the great drivers you can use to create momentum with your email campaign are free. Facebook and Instagram are the big ones. Writing a blog or starting a podcast can also be helpful. LinkedIn and Twitter can be very successful drivers, connecting eyes with your nonprofit online presence but they also come with more rules and you will need to take time and learn what they are. If your attraction funnel is attached to a mature WordPress website, you may consider using the Google Ad Grant, but please research it to make sure you are staying within the guidelines specified by Google.

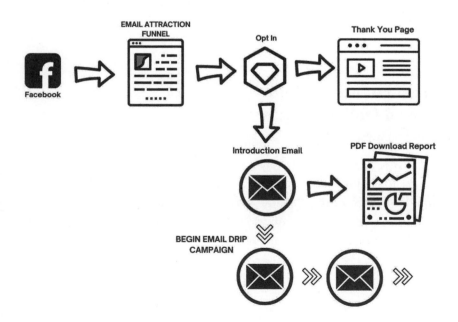

At Sunrise Outreach, a nonprofit that provides food pantries and homeless shelters, their director's goal is to write a new report on their progress every few weeks. As a result, they have a new email-attraction funnel being refreshed constantly, while the previous report becomes an added value they include on future follow-up emails. Before long, Sunrise will be able to have produced enough encouragement to wrap the year, allowing their donors to feel connected constantly to the activities at Sunrise's food pantries and homeless shelters. That's an amazing email drip campaign.

Blueprint 2: The Platinum Donation Funnel

Purpose: Emotional Connection
Action: Small Investment Greater Value

Donation funnels are the center point for income generation with your campaign. They can be driven by all three types of drivers that we talk about in Chapter 12. You can also apply the amazing $10,000 Google Ad Grant to this funnel, which we will discuss in detail in a few pages.

An idea I like is to attach it directly to the "Donate" button on your web page. The email drip campaign feeds into the funding funnel as well and is also the upsell for an affiliate or e-commerce funnel.

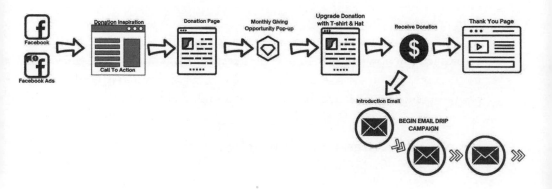

Blueprint 3: Influencer-Driven Funnel

Purpose: One-Time Quick Donor
Action: Intentional Connection

The influencer-driven funnel works in teamwork with an influencer and is a "GoFundMe" type funnel page. The funnel is the communicator and is used to motivate and engage the donor with a simple buy-in. This funnel should also add emails to your email list with the intent to build a relationship with the donor.

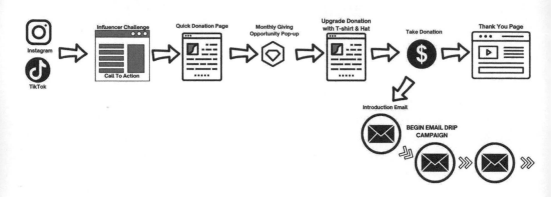

Blueprint 4: Affiliate or E-Commerce Funnel

Purpose: Shopping Funnel
Action: Shopping Supporter

Affiliate or e-commerce funnels need to be set up differently in each state according to nonprofit regulations. You will need to get advice from your CPA. This can be a wonderful way to create income, and you may need to pay tax on income generated, but it is income and can be a lot.

Blueprint 5: Attendance Funnel (Dinner, Concert, etc.)

Purpose: Physical Commitment
Action: Longevity Connection

We encourage every campaign to end in an event like a HERO's Dinner to celebrate everyone who has given. When driven by an attendance funnel

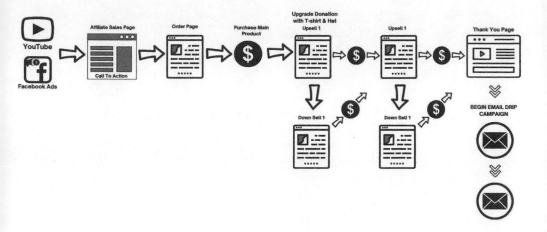

with income-generation strategies, it can double your funding received. You invite everyone near and far who has donated. Those from out of your region can attend virtually. You can attach auctions and awards to increase energy and income. You can even have a carwash driven by an attendance funnel to presell car washes for that day. Like the example below, you can have three levels of donation and carwash services. Let the $$$ roll in.

Blueprint 6: Mini-Class Funnel (Three-part education course based on your value ladder)

Purpose: Education
Action: Entry-Level Value Engagement

Many nonprofits are teeming with education and teaching plans. What have you already created that you could package from a course you are already doing for the local community? Can you break it into three lessons that individually last for 1-3 hours? Drop the prerecorded and edited lessons into a mini-class funnel and *voilà*: You've created a 24/7 fundraiser. Ask for a donation of $49 or $97 to access the course.

While people are watching the course, you can attach affiliate links that are beneficial to the viewer. They can take the next step, and then you have a second source of income. On the last video you spend the last 10 – 20 minutes talking about the wins and possibilities of your nonprofit. You can end with a line such as, "If this course has been a value to you," and then introduce them to the donation funnel.

At the conclusion of the mini class, you can add them to your email drip campaign.

Blueprint 7: Webinar Funnel (High-Cost Course)

Purpose: Education, Coaching, Mentoring
Action: High-Level Value Engagement

The webinar funnel is your "high-ticket" item. This is where you sell your best instructional course. This is a step a mature funnel-building strategy can accomplish. A nonprofit should not start here. Rather, a nonprofit should start with the email-attraction funnel but should reach for the webinar type of funnel as a goal. The webinar funnel is a major commitment and will take planning and dedication.

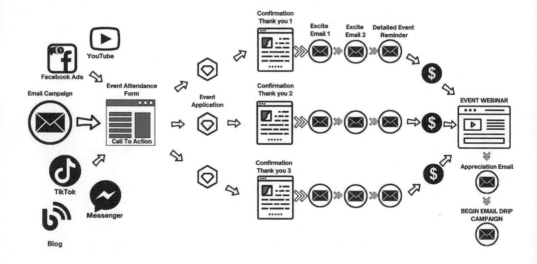

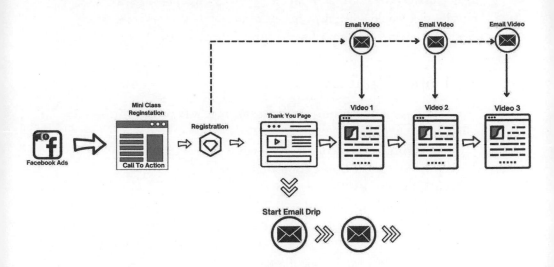

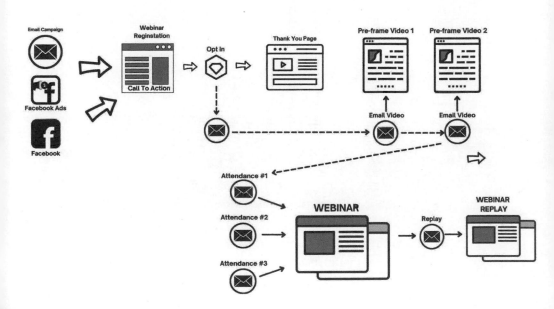

The best driver is going to come from your email list though PPC ads; organic drivers are also highly effective. Once a webinar strategy is being considered, I would schedule it to repeat once for every revenue cycle you operate in whether it is annual, semi-annual, or quarterly.

The Funnel-Value Ladder

Each of the seven blueprints can be seen progressing through the value ladder.

Step 1: **Initial Connection** = Blueprint #1, #6
Step 2: **Emotional Connection** = Blueprint #3
Step 3: **Intentional Connection** = Blueprint #2, #7
Step 4: **Financial Connection** = Blueprint #4
Step 5: **Longevity Connection** = Blueprint #5

The value ladder would look like this:

Blueprint Value Ladder

Take some time and sketch out your next campaign and email it to me here: david@nonprofitonline.net. I'd love to see what you came up with.

WORKING IT OUT

Three Questions

Give yourself a heart check using the "Seven Nevers."

Yes No
- ☐☐ **Am I feeling desperate?**
- ☐☐ **Am I frustrated at my donors or the lack of them?**
- ☐☐ **Am I being cocky about how I'm doing?**
- ☐☐ **Am I feeling too emotional about fundraising?**
- ☐☐ **Do I feel like it does not matter or, perhaps, wonder what the point of it is?**
- ☐☐ **Have I stopped investing in my nonprofit's future?**
- ☐☐ **Have I lost my focus?**

Whom can I speak to about my answers? _____

Where does my value ladder start?

Initial Connection: How many email addresses do I have on my list?
_____

Emotional Connection: Do I know any social influencers? _____
Who? _____

Intentional Connection: My annual budget? $_____ Annual Funding
Goal? _____

Financial Connection: What is a product that matches my nonprofit?
_____

Longevity Connection: If each attending family = $100, how many
households do I want to attend my HERO's e-dinner Event? _____
How many should I invite? _____

CHAPTER 9

ORGANIZING THE WORKFLOW FOR WRITING A HIGH-VALUE ARTICLE

"Either write something worth reading or do something worth writing."
—Benjamin Franklin

It's 6 a.m., and you roll out of bed to start the day. Today is an "information production" morning on your calendar. Two times a week you have committed the hours of 8 a.m. to lunchtime to focus on creating informational stories that will connect readers to your organization. As you start to consider what valuable subject can help readers and address a "pain point" they are facing, the phone rings.

You start the process over. You have decided on the subject; now it's time to write the challenge so you know where you're going. You're halfway through, and your door slams open. Two team members barge in arguing over the way to address a staffing need.

They finally leave. With all your determination and a fresh cup of coffee, you quickly finish the challenge and put together the outline when the phone rings again. As you answer it, a family arrives and asks your secretary if they can speak to you. As you hang up, it rings again, and that's it. Off you go to speak to the family. You will not see your desk again until you're reviewing expenditures that afternoon.

Create Your Writing Bubble

It is important to have a predetermined place you are going to write. When I sat down to write this book, it was during COVID-19 restrictions, so I took our guest bedroom, put the furniture in the garage, set up my desk, and started to write.

It's also imperative as you become an influencer/information provider that you control your creative environment. Create boundaries. Turn off your phone and leave a "Do Not Disturb" note on the door. Speak to any gatekeepers and make sure they understand the importance of this time and ask them to protect the flow of traffic.

Every day when your writing is scheduled, communicate clearly to your team so they know the expectations. It's time to enter your writing bubble. Maybe you already have one at your office, but if there is a need to sequester yourself further, do it.

Block Out Your Time

Time blocking is essential to be successful. Make sure you take the calendar and schedule the time to work on your project.

Connect with Your Editor

Who is going to edit your article or report? I have three people who read my articles and books for flow and connection. I then have a pre-editor review the article. After that, I rewrite the whole piece, and it goes to the editor. Some of you have excellent editing skills. I was speaking to a friend recently who oversees a local nonprofit that is meeting the needs in the homeless population. She is a confident writer who self-edits. I definitely see how that works well for her. However, editing is not my strong suit. In fact, if I had been the editor, you may not have made it to this chapter.

You need to know one thing, though, about great editors. They're truthful, tough, and don't mind hurting your feelings. A great editor is going to cut and adjust your wording and remove what doesn't work in the chapter. You need to have a thick skin.

The many years I was writing and producing music, I had wonderfully talented people editing my work. Still, to this day, the best was Rachael. I have always been a whirlwind of ideas and creative communication, and she would weather the storm and cut into the center of what I was doing and tell me the truth.

"David, that's not working," she would say.

"What do you mean?" I would respond frustratedly. "It's the best part!"

Then she would look at me with determined eyes making sure I got it. "Sure, it's interesting, but it has nothing to do with the point you are making."

"OK, fine," I'd say. "I don't agree, but I'll get rid of it."

I can't think of a time we disagreed, and she didn't end up being right.

If you can do this for yourself, that's great. But if not, you need to find a solid editor for your article ahead of time. As soon as you've finished writing it, forward it to them so they can immediately review it and return it to you for corrections.

Pull Together Your Research

This is where it begins. Do your research as well, then organize your thoughts.

Time to Start Writing

Your goal is to type out 2,000 - 4,000 words. Drop in the illustrations. Now, you just need to put it to work.

Step 1: Write the Challenge; this is your Call to Action. This is where you give the value for staying with you through the article. How do they avoid… or how do they accomplish… or how do they win? End the article with hope, love, joy, kindness. You want readers to be glad they met you, and that feeling of hope is why they will open the next email you send them. You're giving them the feeling of, "You can do this!"

Step 2: Tell the stories that will connect readers to your article. End each with a specific point that relates to the challenge. These are bridge stories, where you will take readers on a journey with you. This allows them to feel your pain or learn your lesson with you. We will go into this a bit further in the next section.

Step 3: Write your first paragraph declaring the Connect. Use engaging wording, desperation, passion, caution, and/or hope. Give readers a reason why they should read your article.

Step 4: Add your limited testimonials and facts backing up your Connect and stories.

Final Step: Declare your title and make sure it has a solid connection or hook.

It's Time to Send it to Your Editor

Remind them to try to have it back as soon as possible.

Let's Design Your Cover

I love using Canva for this. You'll want to keep the cover simple but with a sense of drama.

I can't wait to read your article. Feel free to email it to me for input. I'd love to be a part of your journey as a writer.

WORKING IT OUT

Three Questions

Where and when does the writing take place?

    My Writing Bubble   Writing Schedule

    _____   _____

What are possible subjects I can write about, which are in my nonprofit's niche?

    Topic: _____

    Topic: _____

    Topic: _____

    Topic: _____

    Topic: _____

Whom do I know that could help with the review and editing of my article?

    Name: _____

    Name: _____

    Name: _____

Feel free to post any of your answers on our Facebook group chat for encouraging responses and constructive input.

CHAPTER 10

MULTIPLYING THE EMAIL LIST & WHY IT'S THE BACKBONE OF A NONPROFIT BUDGET

"People who buy products marketed through email spend 138% more than people who do not receive promotional emails."
—Neil Patel

As I stood before Donna, she said, "I think we have 108 emails on the list, and the majority of them are our grant and annual nonprofit funding groups."

There is a principle I heard from online digital marketing guru Russell Brunson. He said, "In the world of digital marketing, 1 email is equal to $1 per month."[17] If that's true, then a smart e-commerce entrepreneur will find his email list equal to his monthly revenue. If an e-commerce enterprise has 10,000 active connections, it is equal to $10,000 gross per month. Wow! What a statistic, and it has proven itself to be true over and over again.

The first time I heard this, it floored me. I had never seen a dollar value given to an email list. That was not part of my training. An email list was used to update one's donors, followers, and team.

If we could translate the digital marketing and business world into donors for our nonprofit, it would be 1 email = $1 per year. (Most nonprofits run on a yearly calendar, unlike e-commerce where everything in a well-run business is operating on a 30-day cycle.)

Let me break this down further.

If 1 email = $1 from a donor who believes in what you are doing, then 100,000 emails = $100,000 in your annual budget. Large nonprofits know this. United Way and the like carefully curate and attend to their email lists every day. They have employees whose only focus is on the care and feeding of "the list."

If Donna knew the $150,000 her nonprofit needed each year could be found in her email list, she could control her budget outcomes with email traffic she is in direct control of.

If 1 active, engaged email subscriber = $1 in Donna's fiscal cycle, then…

- Donna's consistent communication in 75,000 emails would = $75,000.
- If she keeps growing her list, when she is communicating with 150,000 email subscribers, she will have a $150,000 impact on her budget.

Building Your Email List

The number-one way a nonprofit can impact its annual revenue year after year is through the curation and care of its email list.

I would like to reference some of the excellent statistical research (18) Pamela Nelly used on her website Content Wonk. These numbers are used within the data for email automation as she is communicating to e-commerce entrepreneurs. The audience is not what is important here but the tools. Use the same tools and the data will be similar.

Let's examine how she breaks down the numbers that would be required to accomplish such results and how to put a true value on your potential email campaign strength.

1. Determine how many engaged email subscribers you have. Note: "Churn Rate" In the e-commerce world describes the annual

amount of emails that unsubscribe or fall off your active email list. According to GetResponce, about 25%-30% of online business contacts fall off the list in a year.[18] *(Keep reading; nonprofit stats are much better.)*

2. Determine how much revenue you've made from your list over the past year and divide by 12 months.
3. Remember to consider your overhead costs for email production.
4. Now calculate your email revenue. The formula looks like this:

Emails Acquired (- churn rate) + Monthly Revenue (- costs) = Subscriber Value

Let's take a deeper look at the above numbers and translate them into non-profits and donors.

First, how many engaged email subscribers does your organization have? If you don't have a quick number off the top of your head, you could find it by researching the following:

- In the past year, whom (individuals and families) have you emailed for any reason?
- Who volunteered at your nonprofit?
- What businesses have helped, donated, or supplied goods in the past 12 months?
- Who are your neighbors?
- Whom have you hired as a subcontractor or 1099?
- Include your and your team's personal friends and family where appropriate.

Now, here's some really encouraging news. The churn rate is much smaller in a nonprofit than in a business by nature of the passion within the connection. It's often called the "back door" rate in member-driven 501(c)s.

For the last three nonprofit boards on which I served, we averaged an 8%-17% churn, or back door, rate. During one year with the Performing Arts Center my team helped me build in San Diego, it was as low as 6%.

Next, what is your donor revenue from your email communications? You may not know the answer to this question, especially since you are reading this book. That's all right; if you have not used your email list as a revenue stream, then your answer is zero, and next year will reflect 100% growth.

The Three Tiers of Funding

Nonprofits have three tiers of funding:

- Tier One: Immediate Impact Income
- Tier Two: Secondary Supportive Donor Giving
- Tier Three: The "Just in Time" Surprise Donation

As nonprofits, we throw ourselves into the "good" found in the work we are doing. It feeds our soul and gives us meaning. Hearing a "thank you" from those we encounter on our mission is often enough. Therefore, we don't take the time for one of the most important facets in long-term funding, the Tier Two Secondary Support Giving.

Tier One: Immediate Impact Income

These are public and private grants, provided purposefully for a specific project. For a membership organization, it can be monthly or annual dues. For a religious nonprofit, it may be the core giving or "tithes" which are part of the budget.

Tier Two: Secondary Support Giving

This is giving from "the bench." No basketball team can win a championship without a strong bench. Emails are the King of the Bench, the "6th man" in a basketball analogy. The pinch hitter in the baseball game. A well-developed email list can save the game, so to speak. It funds the spaces and holes in the budget. And when a grant fails, it's the emails that bring home the win. I'd go so far as to say, without a strong email growth system in play which is maintaining consistent connection with your "fans" or donors, your finances may not have the strength for the big win.

For many years, we used donation drives and person-to-person fundraisers to build Tier Two into our budget. But then 2020 hit, and suddenly what was already happening behind the scenes came to the forefront. America started connecting almost 100% of the time on the internet. The truth is, in 2021, 92% of Americans still used some type of online connection to create or enhance their relationships. Dating, job interviews, networking, even community arts, sports, and educational activities start with online searches and sign-ups before later connecting in person with someone.

The whole world has shifted, and it's time for us to shift as well. This is the era of nonprofit digital funding.

Tier Three: The Surprise Donation

We also call this the "time and place" support or the "lucky gift." I would say to my children when they were young, "Can you go get the mail? See if there's a $1,000 check in there." Even when I didn't say it, the kids would often walk through the door and shout, "Dad, I think I found your $1,000 check." They would then drop a pile of bills on my desk instead. It stopped being cute after a while.

So often as a nonprofit, we rely on Tier One income and somehow find a way to budget "hope" by thinking Tier Three should be in the annual finance projection. Rather, in my opinion, the most stable support system we can build in this era is found in Tier Two… an amazing, unrelenting, colorful, email campaign.

Is it too much to declare? **Your future is in your email list!** That's right. Building your Tier Two funding through a consistent email campaign will create a financial strength your nonprofit can depend on and your Tier One funding mechanisms can flex with.

I think this is the best way to put it when you have built a strong email list: "Do not worry; you can sleep soundly tonight."

The Power of the Value Ladder

I was sitting with John and Mike after a board meeting they had called me to for consultation. After going through stats and numbers again, John shook his head, looked at me and asked the question I had heard from Gabriel just months before: "Why would anybody outside this small community want to donate to us?"

You may be asking the same question, and the answer is simple: They don't.

But when people connect to the need, this changes. When we create a connecting bridge to them, using stories of experiences, dismantled myths, and lessons learned, then we also begin a relationship where value is created. When they see us as their neighbor across the street, perception changes. We become valuable to them. They have entered the first step of our organization's value ladder.

How could that happen? You could give FREE downloads of important communications and research in which your nonprofit is involved. A food bank might write, "Food Crisis: What 5 Things You Need to Have on Your Shelves." An animal shelter could communicate, "What Secrets Your Cat and Dog Don't Want You to Know." A youth director could offer a download such as, "Three Ways to Let Your Teen Know You Love Them." As soon as the reader enters their email address and asks for a download of your report or blog, you have just started a conversation, AND you have a new, active email recipient on your list.

Imagine sending an invitation to a select, concerned, and engaged part of your Facebook, Instagram, TikTok, or even your Twitter community to read your report. That's millions of active people beyond your local community, and suddenly, your nonprofit has a national reach. With your experience and anecdotes, you are multiplying your value to thousands of people you have never met through your email-attraction funnel.

You have just blown right out of your local community, and you're now making potential new friends all over the world. Now that's exciting! We'll talk more about this in the next chapter where we'll discover the secrets of donor and funding drivers.

One thing must be stated, though. There is a noticeably big and bold line between being relatable and truthful on one side, and manipulative and "salesy" on the other. Everything we communicate to express our truth and our story must be accurate and clear. All of us in the nonprofit world understand how important our reputation is. In some ways, it is our best currency. We must build our entire campaign with a clear, 100% focus on establishing a healthy and warm reputation. In all the editing and building of our drivers, we create a firewall cementing correct communication and building trust.

Finally, what expenses should we be looking at to run an effective donor/email campaign? We have a simple formula that includes the three categories of expenses you'll have: Resources + Manpower + Knowledge = The Win!

You may want to roll your eyes and grunt, "Doesn't it always come down to resources, manpower, and knowhow?" But hear me out. You may have resources you didn't know were available or manpower that may be hiding, or most importantly, knowledge downloads that may be easier than you realize.

Resources: If you go online to www.NonprofitOnline.net, you may download all our recommended tools and programs which will allow you to more simply automate much of the process. That would be a good start. Yes, you will need to build your ads (though we can point you toward templates available for you to re-script), write your storylines, and create your hooks, but we are here to help. We have many YouTube "how to" ideas and a vibrant Facebook community to brainstorm with you, and you'll grow into the process.

Manpower: Once you have set up your systems, you can manage your campaign with a three-person team:

Person One: Copywriter—Writes your "copy" or stories.
Person Two: Funnel Builder—Builds your funnels and ads. (This is not so complicated once you know how to access the templates we provide you.)
Person Three: Administrator—Oversees and organizes the email list and makes sure the systems are delivering your messages on time.

Knowledge: We have created an educational channel on YouTube called "Nonprofit Online" for your quick learning. You can view it, subscribe to it, and recommend it to your team and volunteers just by copying and clicking links to content you find beneficial. Our videos helpfully point you in the right direction taking each step piece by piece so you can be confident with your online strategy. Our Facebook community is also available for you to engage with other nonprofit leaders.

Also, each app or program we recommend (and we have carefully searched out the best in each field) provides its own education and helpful support. They will be a financial investment for you but worth every penny.

WORKING IT OUT

Three Questions

If 1 email = $1/year, then how many emails do I need on my nonprofit's list for a healthy Tier Two income?

$_____$ = $_____$ emails on my list

What is a subject your nonprofit could write about that reflects its niche?

_____

Whom do I know that has these skills or can learn them?

Copywriter _____
Funnel Builder _____
Administrator _____

CHAPTER 11

MAPPING THE DRIVERS & FUNNELS SO THEY WILL ENGAGE DONORS

"A little imagination combined with massive action goes a long way."
—**Grant Cardone**

The big question is: How much can a donation funnel net a nonprofit? This is a great question, and the numbers are supported by research. However, have you ever seen an attached legal notice like the one below?

*These results are not typical, and your experience will vary based upon your effort, education, business model, and market forces beyond our control. We make no earnings claims or return on investment claims, and you may not make your money back."

There is a reason why a notice like this appears at the bottom of every communication about income, funding, finance, ads, books, and offers. Though what I am writing about throughout this book is not what is typically seen as financial advice but rather marketing strategy; it is statistics and advice on how your nonprofit can alter its income. So, I must refer you to the above statement and remind you of what I wrote in the preface.

The 100% Truth

You want me to be 100% truthful, don't you? Then this is it: There is not a foolproof plan available to you. Your success is based on your work ethic and strategy. It is limited by your knowledge of the marketplace and experience.

In 2014, it was unheard-of for nonprofits to use digital marketing tools for email-attraction and donation funnels. Then a struggling camp director in eastern Canada did something unheard-of for nonprofits.

Tyler and Janet ran a small summer camp in Ottawa, Canada. They were just covering the bills. It would not have taken much for the budget to run out before the end of the year.

Out of a struggle to find something new that would allow his reach to increase and income to grow, Tyler read a book called *Dotcom Secrets* by Russell Brunson. He started studying digital marketing tactics and sales funnels in his spare time and built a strategy based on what he learned. Soon, he created his first nonprofit click funnel and attached the drivers.

As a result, by the next year, he and his team saw some limited growth at the camp: 300 new registrations for summer camp. In the second year, they added 1,500 youth. By year three of educating himself and using funnels as a funding and attendance-driving mechanism, they were $600,000 above budget. After another two years, they saw $1 million from just one funnel.

At Nonprofit Online we have created titles that celebrate this kind of success:

Funnel Genius has raised $25,000 with one funnel.
Funnel Artist has raised $500,000 with one funnel.
Funnel Master has raised $1,000,000 with one funnel.

Tyler was our first nonprofit funnel builder recognized as a Funnel Master in our Nonprofit Online community. He proved to many that they can now reimagine new expectations with donors and rethink the funding limitations they once believed their organizations had.

Your situation may be different from Tyler's. Your motivations and drive may be different. He had to find a way to reach beyond the walls and limitations that were unique to him. You will need to do the same for your nonprofit.

Digital platforms like your website, the building of donation funnels, email automation, and social influencer platforms are the biggest part of being a nonprofit with a successful online presence. But there is a very important piece that completes your online strategy. There must be a vehicle that draws your future donors to the above platforms. We call these motivators "drivers."

Unboxing Drivers?

How do you reach beyond the walls as a nonprofit? You may have built your funnels and have a dynamic website, but do you need more than that? Yes. A funnel, like a website, is static without something to influence viewers to see it. The tools we use to make this happen are called "drivers."

Though there are many ways other professionals may categorize and label drivers, I am going to adopt three simple categories used consistently throughout digital marketing. They are Organic, Paid, and Hybrid Drivers

Organic Drivers: An organic driver is a free social platform or engagement tool that is able to draw your potential donor to click onto your site. Below is a workflow that includes many of the more popular organic drivers.

Step One: Write a **blog** with links to your funnel.

Step Two: **Email** and **Messenger** the blog to your entire list asking everyone to share the email to at least five friends.

Step Three: Post the blog on **LinkedIn** with links to your funnel.

Step Four: **Tweet, Snapchat**, and **TikTok** about the blog to all your followers.

Step Five: Use the blog as a script for a **YouTube** upload with links to your funnels.

Step Six: Post clips on **Facebook** and **Instagram** of the YouTube video with a link to your funnel.

Step Seven: Reach out to **podcasts** and **vloggers** to interview you about your nonprofit. You can use the blog as context.

Write a new blog and do it again… momentum is building, and your nonprofit is starting to spread its wings. Check out this blueprint with organic drivers pushing an email-attraction funnel. You will not want to use all of these, but pick and choose what are the best drivers to be able to maintain over the long run.

Paid Drivers: Just like the name implies, these are the paid ads you use to bring people to your funnel or website. You can make great gains using these, but as a warning, the large companies like Google and Facebook often change their accessibility and effectiveness. These changes may not affect the multimillion-dollar corporation advertising on Facebook, but they could be very frustrating to the smaller nonprofit trying to advertise.

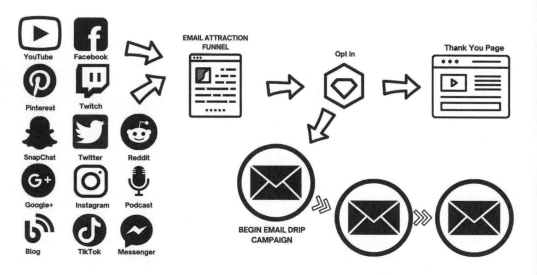

The benefit to using paid drivers is that, if it is done well, you will receive a multiplication of responses to your funnel and website views. It takes constant vigilance, effective A/B testing, and learning the language of hooks and stories. Mastering the art of the upskill is also important so you can effectively capture the imagination of your target audience.

Many digital marketers will often consider using only one or two paid advertising campaigns, using them as a multiplier to their already running organic drivers. I also know that, as nonprofits, we can always layer the paid ads as needed. Here are a series of paid drivers for your consideration:

Nonprofits' most popular driver is the effective use of the $10,000 a month **Google Ad Grant**. It must be focused on your domain name and managed well, but you can use your website as a driver into the funnel as well. The cost is the management of the account, whether you use an employee or hire a marketing company to do it.

Facebook PPC Advertising is also immensely popular because of the response rate and algorithm that it uses. This allows you to use pinpoint accuracy in choosing your potential future donors with a lot of data to help with the follow-up. One of the great benefits is that you may be having thousands of Facebook users scrolling past your ad, gaining you free recognition. You only pay when they click on the ad itself.

YouTube Advertising: This can be tricky. Remember, you will not be seen by the premium customers, only by YouTube's basic users. BUT… You can research having a YouTube influencer represent or promote your nonprofit and link to your webpage or funnel site. It may cost a few hundred dollars, but it's worth it if the influencer is driving viewers to your funnel. Just study the ROI.

Almost all social media platforms have the ability to sell paid advertising space where you can drive your funnel site, but you will need to choose which ones are best for you.

Don't forget direct advertising on community forums and newsletters that are within your niche. Here's a graph showing a donation funnel blueprint with paid drivers.

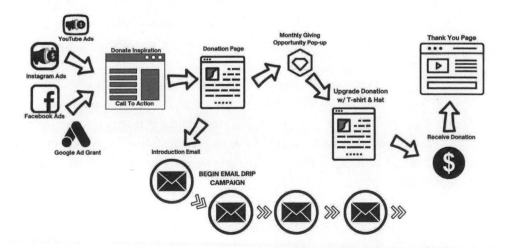

Hybrid Drivers: There are numerous paid programs that allow you to enhance your organic drivers. An example of this is when you take a free platform like Facebook and pay for Facebook to "push" your post. Paying Facebook to push organic marketing is considered using a hybrid driver.

If smartly used, hybrid drivers are less expensive than paid drivers and can be highly effective. Though in many cases they take an extra step in your strategy, they are often worth it. You can also use the hybrid or "add on" platforms as a way to gather further information about who is responding to your nonprofit.

For example, if you like your LinkedIn platform and know the specific niche you are reaching out to, you can add on your **LinkedIn Navigator** program to research professionals that match your ideal donor. The next step would be to integrate the Navigator program with a great program called **Dux-Soup,** and then direct Dux-Soup's AI to write messages for you using the LinkedIn Navigator contact list.

Don't Overdo It

It's easy to look at all the options, become overwhelmed with the choices, and just stop. One of the most effective campaigns I have seen was put together by a brand-new funnel builder we are going to call Chet. He used a single driver and focused it into a simple e-commerce (sales) funnel.

His campaign blueprint was as simple as this:

Chet heard about funnels, and while studying them over a number of weeks, discovered that almost all items for sale on the internet offer affiliate programs.

An affiliate program is an agreement between a store and someone like you. You apply for an affiliate number with (as an example) Amazon (or a thousand other vendors), and they give you a number that you attach to your funnel. When the item is purchased, you get an affiliate fee, which may range from as little as 2% of the purchase price to other items that will pay you 40-50%, or even higher.

Chet soon built his first funnel and launched it. Because he couldn't think of another way to drive the funnel, he just bought Facebook ads as his only driver.

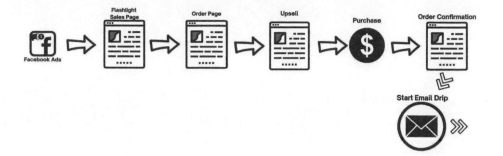

Six days later he looked at his return and only had made a couple thousand dollars. He immediately found a second product and attached it to his next funnel, and seven days after launching his first site, he launched his second. This funnel was a bit better but still disappointing.

For six weeks in a row, Chet built a new funnel for each new product he could sell as an affiliate product. Each week he saw stronger returns. On week five, he had a great return and put over $100,000 away in his account.

On the next attempt, he marketed a military-grade, hand-sized flashlight. He attached a picture of a person lighting up the whole side of a hill with it and built his funnel. He had hit the jackpot. Seven days later, the funnel had broken $1 million in gross revenue.

The point of Chet's story is that you don't have to use a lot of drivers. Just find the one you can use best and put it to work.

WORKING IT OUT

Three Questions

Which funnels will work for my nonprofit, and what goals should I set?

	2022	2023	2024	2025	2026
Donor Funnel (Email List)	___K	___K	___K	___K	___K
Quick-Connect Funnel	$___K	$___K	$___K	$___K	$___K
Funding Funnel	$___K	$___K	$___K	$___K	$___K
E-Commerce Funnel	$___K	$___K	$___K	$___K	$___K
Attendance Funnel	$___K	$___K	$___K	$___K	$___K

Which staff members can work with me?

	Name	Skill	Hr./wk.
1.	_____	_____	_____
2.	_____	_____	_____
3.	_____	_____	_____

Which volunteers are available, and what skills would be helpful?

	Name	Skill	Hr./wk.
1.	_____	_____	_____
2.	_____	_____	_____
3.	_____	_____	_____

CHAPTER 12

BUILDING YOUR FUNNEL CAMPAIGN BUDGET

"Becoming rich is hard.
Staying broke is hard.
Choose your hard."
—Eric Worre

You may be asking, "So, David, how much is using digital marketing going to cost my nonprofit?" Let's review several separate online revenue streams available to you. Afterward, we will look at some of the tools you will need for your success and why you should use them.

Because there are hundreds of money-making ideas from flipping products to creating e-book downloads, I filtered out things that do not sustain themselves and do not have the ability to provide residual income. This way, once you have taken the pain to create the platform, you only need to manage it while you are keeping your focus on your nonprofit.

Here are some of my favorites:

Webinars: If done well, these can provide an unlimited income stream. Most nonprofits already help and educate people within their charity's specific niche. They have already created a curriculum which they confidently communicate to others. Now they just need to change the platform from a room with the circle of chairs to a webinar presentation. Then they launch it with a promising driver strategy and price point—and "boom."

Donation Funnels: We have already spent a lot of time talking about these. Though they are completely dependent on your drivers, in truth, the sky's the limit.

The Email List: This comes down to two skills: Can you articulate the need well, and can you create a great value exchange?

Teaming Fundraising With Funnels: You can use funnels to multiply the ROI of your current fundraisers. I've shown you how a $1,000 carwash can raise $5,000 using an attendance funnel or how using a funnel to market and presell tickets to your gala, dessert banquet, or even a concert can greatly increase your success. Every fundraising season, you just pull out the funnel you used last time, freshen it up, and reuse.

Affiliate Links: These are a popular and effective funding choice you can use strategically in your social media posts and website. You can include them in your podcast description, your blogs and newsletters, and video content. Emails can also be an appropriate place to use them, but be careful to know the rules and limitations of your email server so your email will not be sent to spam. Once you have matured your affiliate strategy, you can budget up to four figures a week in income.

- I love digital products as affiliate links. They often pay out a larger percentage, like 20% all the way to 60% of the purchase. In contrast, product sales usually only pay out 2%-4%. Also, digital product contracts will often pay out residually for the lifetime of the user. Since the list is long and detailed, the subject of affiliate links and strategies could be a whole book in itself. I have included a few recommended products in the next points, and we also go into greater detail with more options on our YouTube channel, Nonprofit Online.
- Amazon is a strong second just because of the way it is set up. It pays you a small percentage (.5% – 2%+) on 100% of all purchases within a 24-hour period of time after the purchaser uses your link to enter their platform. Your nonprofit will still receive an affiliate commission even if the buyer ends up paying for a product completely non-related to the product your nonprofit recommended. Why? You may ask.

Amazon gives you credit for being the reason the shopper even came to them to shop.

- Fiverr is an online marketplace for freelance services. The company provides a platform for freelancers to offer services to customers worldwide. When you recommend Fiverr.com as a member of its affiliate program, and a person uses its platform, you can get up to $150 or a 10% revenue share for up to 12 months. If you've ever used them as a service, you should write a blog or post about your experience and include the link. Then, "let it ride."
- Website hosting companies make up another great sector. Bluehost, HostGator, and GoDaddy all pay out a set fee. WordPress is an exception because it is a free platform. Who is your domain hosting site? Look into its affiliate program and then brag about it in an email or social post and add the link.

I think you get the idea here. There are a ton of options out there. Affiliate programs are a great way to help people that are looking for recommendations and, at the same time, bring in a new revenue stream for you.

Merchandise: This comes down to your active online engagement and marketing skill. It has great scaling ability if you study your clientele and lean your ad spending into their passions and spending habits.

I recommend using an online "product satisfaction" business that will print your T-shirts, hats, mugs, and other fun merchandise and fulfill the orders when they come in. This way, all you need to do is create and include the link to the product in your online postings and forget it.

Doing all the product fulfillment on your own will bring you more profit, but then you are dealing with returns and customer satisfaction issues as well as boxing and shipping. Wouldn't you rather just work on your nonprofit and leave the rest for someone else? I would, and I do.

Advertising Sponsors: As your blogs, podcasts, or posts gain a following, so does the attraction associated with your organization. Success breeds success, and a business standing beside your nonprofit brings you a status boost. You are not asking them for a handout but rather offering to help them by giving their business the opportunity to advertise with you.

I highly recommend building relationships with other businesses local to you specifically for creating ad revenue. This becomes easier the bigger you grow your email list and online platform. As you become more confident in your platform, your ask for advertising will become more comfortable.

Nonprofit E-Commerce Funnel: An average e-commerce site or sales funnel will give you a $1-to-$2 ($1 advertising to $2 return) ratio. Pick the right product and market it to the right audience, and you have a solid income stream for your nonprofit.

How Easy Is It?

It's not easy. Like everything in life, there is a learning curve. It is important to understand that, as an individual and as a nonprofit, you will need to crawl before you walk, and walk before you run.

Spencer Mecham is a YouTube coach who spends a lot of time building affiliate educational tools. Although he has had great success over the last few years, his journey did not start there. It started with him newly married with his first child on the way and living in a tiny home. He found a small space in his cold, concrete basement. Every day after work, he would spend time trying to figure out how to make money online with affiliate marketing and building funnels. He lacked coaching and tutorials but kept trying to figure it out. For eight months he banged his head, making only a few hundred dollars a month.

Spencer was self-taught and didn't have much in the way of support, yet he persevered. Suddenly, after eight months he had a post blow up to over 500,000 views, and he was off and running. Now he mentioned in a recent post that affiliate marketing netted him over $3,000,000 this last year. (Check out his amazing story at https://www.youtube.com/watch?v=M3eh4gQByBA)

As you see in Spencer's case, you have to be persistent and show "pig-headed discipline." If you're going to post a blog, make sure you are being consistent and do it every week for a year. If your nonprofit is going to launch a YouTube channel, post 36 videos without blinking and then evaluate and post weekly for 12 months. The same goes for any type of social media.

Momentum and income arrive because of the cumulative effect of layered posts. One post brings in $100, but 50 posts that are just as frustratingly ineffective bring in $5,000. See how the accumulation of posts and time works. It comes down to being consistent and never stopping with upskilling and creating value.

Cost Comparisons

Shifting your organization to a strong online strategy involves considering many financial aspects. The costs for start-up expenses and then creating momentum vary widely depending on what blueprint you choose. For instance, are you going to focus on website tools and drivers only? Do you want to unleash funnels upon the world and use organic drivers? Does your budget allow for paid advertising and, if so, how much?

No matter how much work goes into saving you money with your initial investment, you will still need to step up and make the "call for the win." Keep in mind one thought, though: Count the cost before you start and don't flinch.

Below are the items you need to budget for.

Education

All well-developed programs should come with plenty of instruction. YouTube is also an effective free educational tool as well. Your biggest need at the beginning is getting the books that will allow you to build your overall strategy. I hope you feel this book is a positive first step, but I would like you to also consider books from two other authors:

1. *Dotcom Secret* series by Russell Brunson. Russell is one of the founders of funnel technology and strategy. Even his fiercest competitors admit that his educational tools are, "bar none," the absolute best in the industry. His ability to create frameworks for you to use is exceptional. After reading *Pivot or Die*, his books should be next. (LINK:https://www.dotcomsecrets.com?cf_affiliate_id=3020549 &affiliate_id=3020549 Here is my affiliate link so you can get a free copy with shipping and handling)

2. *The Ultimate Sales Machine* by Chet Holmes is the only and last book you ever need on how to exchange value for income. If you can understand his sales language that is meant for corporations and businesses needing to find customers, and which is filtered through the framework of a nonprofit leader needing to discover donors, you will be glad you read his book.

3. ***Demystifying Fundraising Funnels*** by David Higgins. Nonprofit Online has created a discount team package that will provide for you coaching, tools and a group bundle package of this book. This is where your team needs to start. It will explain the exchange of terminologies and enable your team to understand digital marketing and for-profit language used in digital marketing. (LINK: www.fundraisingfunnels.org)

Funnel Building

I can recommend multiple funnel-building programs with prebuilt templates available. My team has helped me review them, and out of the 42 funnel options we examined, we have found our favorites.

ClickFunnels 2.0 (launching March 2022) is my top recommendation. It was designed by brilliant software engineer Todd Dickerson and his team which is ideal for Nonprofit Online so we could provide an all-in-one platform created and affordable for nonprofits. It has all the needed integrations within its workflow, with more being added as the need is seen. It is created to meet your nonprofit's needs as you venture online and is built to scale with your learning curve. You would have no need for email servers, automations, phone, text options, etc. All these things are built into it. You can launch your funnels for under a $100 a month, and if you want to build your email list on your platform you can grow quite large. It is well worth checking out.

WordPress is the no-frills leader. It is more cumbersome and has no extra frills other than the apps you can add on, but in the long run, you save money. You can get a full funnel up and going for about $89/month with all the integrations that ClickFunnels provides, but without the community or educational tools.

Website

You have many website options, and there is a high chance that you already have a website for your charity. I have built websites on various platforms including Wix and Squarespace, but I would like to encourage you to consider a WordPress platform for your site. It is very Google-search friendly and works in accordance with many platforms when attaching funnels to the back end like this: www.domainname.org/funnel id.

Drivers

As a quick review, your driver strategy has three parts. **Organic Drivers** that will create momentum, and the **$10,000 a month Google Ad Grant** which is the best of organic drivers. Once you have income coming in, you might invest in the programs that will enhance your organic drivers and drop the lever on the **Hybrid Platforms.** Finally, multiply the response to your already successful funnel page with **Paid Ads**. Now it's all over but the high fives.

Let's look deeper into each driver.

Organic Drivers

We start with the **Organic Drivers**. We suggest you begin with what you are already active on and build off those platforms. Streamline the branding, pictures, and wording between platforms. Create systems so your team can do this quickly and simply. It is important that your message carries from your posts through to your funnel and website.

As of the writing of this book there are 103 "high user" social media platforms, and new ones are being created every month. Many top organic drivers that I like are LinkedIn, Facebook, Instagram, podcasts, blogs, YouTube, TikTok, Pinterest, Reddit, Twitter, Snapchat, Twitch, and Trello. And then, there are the new and trying-hard-to-enter-the-mainstream grouping: Byte, Zynn, and Triller, plus many more.

Emails are the king of organic drivers and can efficiently bring donors to your funnels. Your email attraction funnels in and of themselves will bring in more email addresses each month, creating an infinite resource.

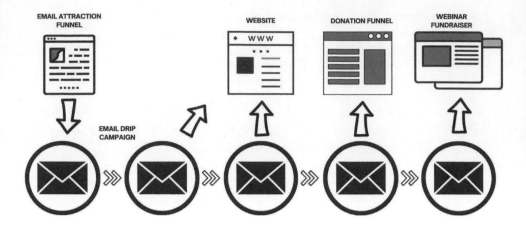

EMAIL ATTRACTION FUNNEL · WEBSITE · DONATION FUNNEL · WEBINAR FUNDRAISER · EMAIL DRIP CAMPAIGN

Email Servers

It is important to choose the right email server that will fit your long-range goals. I have personally found this frustrating. For instance, when I find a great service like AWeber, it won't integrate with the funnel hosting program I want. Or I have chosen an email server like Active Campaign that has amazing features but does not have an SMTP server. Then I would need to pay for Zapier to integrate it with a singular SMTP Server, which is a third expense. (Maybe by the time you read this, Active Campaign will have fixed the problem.)

We have found that Mail Chimp is a decent all-around email server to use when working with programs that ask for email integration like ClickFunnels. It may feel a bit clunky to work with, but it's free till you have 2,000 emails in your system.

If you are looking at programs like Active Campaign or AWeber, you will be working with a program that is like a new Mercedes-Benz. Many within the funnel-building community highly recommend these programs, but they do come with a hefty price tag. This is something you will need to decide on.

Fortunately, there is Idaho-based company, ClickFunnels, or French company with a slightly less integrated program, Sendinblue. They both operate more like a 2022 Honda Accord or Subaru Outback. They are clean and functional and come with some bells and whistles but without the clout and special features like in other programs. The question is, "Do

Email Automation Servers

Email Automation Servers	FREE Options	CRM	Web/Funnel Builder	Scheduling (like Calendly)	Phone & Text	Supports Affiliate Links in Emails
FunnelFlow	over 50,000	YES	YES	YES	BOTH	YES
MailChimp	up to 2000				TEXT	LIMITED
SendGrid	100/day				TEXT	YES
Sparkpost	30 days					
Mailgun	90 days					
GetResponce	30 days		YES		TEXT	YES
Sendinblue	300/day	YES	YES	YES		YES
ConstantContact	60 days				TEXT	
ActiveCampaign	14 days	YES	YES		TEXT	
AWeber	up to 500		YES		TEXT	YES
ConvertKit	up to 1,000					YES
MailerLight	14 days		YES			
SendLane	14 days				TEXT	YES

you need those features offered in the bigger, more expensive programs?" Are you building an e-commerce and digital marketing business, or rather a donation funnel to support your nonprofit?

The $10,000/month Google Ad Grant

One amazing and popular opportunity is the $10,000 a month nonprofit **Google Ad Grant**. The easy part is the application. Filling it out correctly and following the rules takes only 15 minutes. After the application is done, the tricky part hits. There are so many qualifications and ways to be kicked out of the program that only 2% of those who get the grant use more than $250.

The key is to have a skilled person who knows SEO and Google Ad Words on your team. This is not a usual skillset for a nonprofit. Fortunately for you, we love the nonprofit Google Ad Grant and have invested in the education and skills to teach it to you. You have multiple choices:

- You can have a team member learn the Google Ad Grant skillset thru our "Nonprofit Online Webinar Series." This way you can be self-reliant.

- Another option is for the Nonprofit Online team to manage it for your nonprofit.
- Also, there are many Certified Google Ad Grant Marketing companies that Google has vetted; they can be found at https://www.google.com/grants/get-help/certified-professional-agencies. Research this page before you make your decision. There are marketing companies that are listed that are specific to regions like Canada, England, or Australia and other international companies that specialize and offer many extra benefits.

Consider what a $120,000 a year grant that is driving internet traffic to your nonprofit events and funding campaigns can do for you!

Paid Ads are powerful, but nonprofits should not rely on them. Instead, nonprofits should use them only to boost their strategic fundraising events or help create momentum for a particular funnel. Understanding how ad template programs work can greatly enhance your effectiveness and speed up your learning curve.

I encourage you to search YouTube and research the exact platform you are looking to advertise with. For example, "How do I advertise on Instagram" or "What are PPC ad strategies for Facebook." It's all there only a keystroke away.

Ad template programs are an especially useful tool, but deciding where to put your money is key. Here is a list for a social media plan of attack for the year ahead. This list is in order of the number of active users according to Tech.co.[19]

- Facebook
- Instagram
- TikTok
- Pinterest
- Reddit
- Twitter
- LinkedIn
- Snapchat
- YouTube

When we are running a campaign for a nonprofit organization, we often start with a $20/day **PPC Facebook Ad** strategy starting in week two or three.

José is a dedicated board treasurer of a homeless charity. His eyes almost popped out of his head the first time I suggested this to his board, and I could see the arguments rising to the surface of his brain like a tsunami.

Before he spoke, I did something I often do at this point in a conversation. I handed him five single dollar bills. The tsunami froze out of pure curiosity. I then asked him to hand me one dollar. As he did, I took it from his hand and replaced it with three new dollars. I asked him again for another dollar. This time I replaced it with a $5 note.

Then I asked him if he would give me a dollar every day if I kept replacing it with a larger denomination. He smiled and said, "Yeah, I guess I would."

It's the same thing with Facebook Ads. If done correctly, they can reap a continued income greater than the investment.

This is why I recommend you wait until after the organic connection is made to be sure of your wording and hook. Then, follow it up with a daily review of the PPC statistics until you become confident and delegate the daily review to your team member. In the next chapter we dive into this process in more detail.

Content Creation

So, now you have everything ready to go. You just need to put something on the pages. Following are a few of the programs we use here at Targeted Marketing Group and Nonprofit Online.

Video Capture: We recommend using a free program that is easy to learn called OBS project: http://obsproject.com/.

Video Editing: Everybody loves editing the footage in Adobe and for good reason. The downside to Adobe is that it is another monthly expense. We love and highly encourage you to check out DaVinci Resolve17 by Blackmagic Design. You can start for free, it's easy to learn, and the product you end up with can be very professional.

Design: The most highly regarded software by many in the industry is Canva. It's the best branding and design shop we can recommend. From creating thumbnails to logos, LinkedIn banners to video introductions, business cards to Facebook Ads, it's our best recommendation. The great thing is it has a free version so you can dive in and let loose your creativity.

Product Placement: PlaceIt is an easy-to-use platform for putting your reports, e-books, and logos in the hands and on the clothing of incredibly happy people. You can quickly upload your Canva design into PlaceIt and then insert it onto a mug being held by a model. Likewise, you can take a Canva-designed book cover and insert it into one of several hundred pictures of people reading to make it look as though they are reading your book or report. The same concept also goes for T-shirts, hoodies, and hats. Then you download the picture with your logo onto your desktop or file until you're ready to place it into your funnel.

Support Options

We recommend the following companies based on simplicity, reliability, and price:

Payments – Stripe
Calendar and Scheduling – Calendly
Mapping Funnels – Funnelytics
Bookkeeping – TheNonprofitBookkeeper.com
Photography and Video Stock – Shutterstock and Vimeo.com

Just a Quick Review

Your expenses generally lie in three categories: education, funnel building, and drivers. Each is a unique and important part to your campaign. Once the initial investment is made to start the process rolling, your strategy is always to build out of earnings and be in continual profit. For the nonprofits I consult we have a minimum requirement for ROI (Return On Investment). It is $2 earned for every $1 spent. We start every campaign, though, with a much higher goal which is to receive $5 for every $1 spent and then reach beyond that number.

Please log onto NonprofitOnline.net for more details and links to platforms and educational material.

WORKING IT OUT

Three Questions

What resources do you have available in your budget?

_____

_____

How fast do you want to scale? _____

What skillsets do you need to subcontract? _____

CHAPTER 13

INSPECTING YOUR NEW FUNNEL CAMPAIGNS

"Quality is not an act; it's a habit."

—Aristotle

Many years ago, my good friend, Lieutenant Junior Grade Joshua Menzel, and I were driving from San Diego to Pullman, WA. He was getting married in four days, and we were so excited that we decided to drive the 22 hours straight through. That trip cemented a relationship that continues to this day.

A few years later, the newly promoted LT,03 Menzel was serving on the board of a nonprofit with me. We were walking out of an intense board meeting where we had been discussing the details of the numerous teams I was leading and a capital campaign we were about to begin. I was getting frustrated. As we descended the stairs, he turned to me and said the phrase I've carried with me for the rest of my life:

"David," he said, "You won't get what you don't inspect."

Now a captain, Josh has had to live by those words, duty station after duty station. I have watched as he has commanded ships of all sizes and now serves at a command overseeing a U.S. Navy base. Those seven very practiced words have proven themselves again and again: "You won't get what you don't inspect!"

This is equally as true with creating funnels. As you are learning a new way of raising funds, you need to be doing constant inspection and improvement. You have to "know to grow," and simply setting it up and forgetting about it is not going to work in your favor.

Ideally, once you have created your funnel, you should create a team member who can provide a daily review. They should report to you once or twice a week so you are aware of and can help with needed adjustments.

Russell Brunson encourages all his students to build a funnel, create the drivers, and keep inspecting and improving their system until it breaks a million dollars. A million dollars may not be your specific goal as a nonprofit leader, but the concept is the same.

The Part-Time Funnel Builder

Some of us have the privilege to have a full-time fundraiser or grant writer on our staff, but those are the minority. For those who raise funds on a part-time basis only, have hope. It takes about two hours to build a quality funnel. It takes another two hours to set up your drivers and about one hour a day to review and correct your ads and drivers.

I recommend doing a quick assessment of the time you invest annually into your fundraising. Include both the cost of doing the fundraiser and the cost of having you distracted from your nonprofit focus. Once you have assessed the hours and the dollars, consider the funnel schedule. It can be done in 5-10 hours per week, and much of it is able to be delegated, with you inspecting the outcomes and suggesting course corrections.

The 30-Day Inspection Schedule

Here is a suggested workflow for inspections once a funnel is launched:

Day 1- Launch the funnels and organic drivers.
Day 2 - Review stats and make any adjustments.

Day 3 - Launch second set of organic drivers.

Day 4 - Review stats and make any adjustments.

Day 5 - Do split tests and correct both funnels and drivers.

Day 8 - Launch party!!!

Day 9 - Review stats and make any adjustments.

Day 10 - Review stats and make any adjustments.

Day 11 - Review stats and make any adjustments.

Day 12 - Do split tests and correct both funnels and drivers.

Day 15 - Launch the PPC Ads and review or delegate the daily review.

Day 17 - Review stats.

Day 19 - Do split tests and correct ad drivers.

Day 23 - Launch fresh ads.

Day 25 - Review stats.

Day 27 - Do split tests and correct ad drivers.

Day 31 - One-month review.

The Young Upskill—Don't Call Me Old!

My life has been a journey of learning, re-learning, and re-learning all over again.

I wanted to learn the Māori war dance, the Haka. Born in Palmerston North, New Zealand, you would think it should have been a natural internal gift... but nope. To this day, I still feel so uncoordinated and disconnected from it. I love seeing others dance it. I even get emotional when I see it done well. I love it, and it makes me smile.

I'm proud of my homeland, but the Haka still doesn't feel quite right when I try to dance it. I know it's because I'm comparing myself to the 16- and 22-year-old athletes I see dancing it on YouTube when I'm 50. The same may be true for you when it comes to digital marketing. It is different from what we have always known, but that doesn't mean we can't learn how to use it to fund our nonprofits.

We are approaching a big change in fundraising culture. The old is tactile, and the new is digital. Yes, we can converge them when needed, but the future is online, and the leaders willing to educate themselves and learn the language of digital marketing will find more open doors and raise more funds.

We learn, we build funnels, we inspect funnels. It ends with amazing new donors and fresh income filling the needs of our organizations. You can do this, and I'm here to cheer you and your nonprofit on.

WORKING IT OUT
Three Questions

What is the date of the next free Funnel Strategy Webinar?
____/____/____

Have I called for a FREE Consultation yet? _____

What is a "Nonprofit Online Mastermind Weekend"?
_____
_____

CHAPTER 14

A COMMUNITY OF NONPROFIT FUNNEL BUILDERS

"There are countless people that have gone before you."
—Lucas Lee-Tyson

Nonprofit Online is not the pioneer. We are standing on the shoulders of amazing funnel builders like Tyler and others who went before us. We know who the first ones were, such as Russell Brunson, to venture into the world of digital marketing and funnel building. They came back with tested systems for the nonprofit world. We know them because they are the ones who came striding back into town, weather-beaten and looking for water, but the words on their lips made our hearts race: "There's gold in them thar hills!"

In 2008, the pioneers in digital marketing started figuring out where technology was taking the internet commerce and online revenue markets. By 2014, the roads were built and ready for use by us city folk.

The template and ad platforms became easily usable by 2015, and that's when the first nonprofits (except for a few early birds) started moving in one at a time. In 2020, we saw the market shift dramatically, then settle. Now that shift has become the online law of exchange: the trade of money for value. This cultural shift is ready for the nonprofit world to fully engage in and build our funding future upon.

We are at a point of decision. As nonprofits, can we let go of the frustration of begging for funds and pandering to institutional donors and step into something new? We have a marketplace where we can trade value for the attention of donors and create funding from the influencer marketplace, not by asking for help, but by providing anecdotes, ideas, and experience that will trade value for community.

We have spoken about those who have already entered this new nonprofit funding culture. Here are a few honorable mentions I thought would be encouraging.

Case Study: Social Service Nonprofit

Elizabeth Shores raised enough funding in ONE funnel to start bringing clean water to African villages.

Patrick and Elizabeth Shore run a nonprofit called Untapped Shores.[20] They provide clean water and business opportunities for women and their families in Africa.

The problem is traditional fundraisers are so expensive, and they were exhausted and tired from chasing every donation. All they knew were the brick-and-mortar fundraisers and silent auctions. They wanted a new way to stand apart. They had 200 villages in just one country waiting for support. They needed to revolutionize their strategy, and fast.

When first approached about using funnels for a funding avenue, it took the conversation of a friend who already had seven-figure successes in building and running e-commerce funnels. Instead of just donating to Untapped Shores, she helped Elizabeth and Patrick plan out their own funnel.

Their hook was, "Are You Ready to Make History?" They added thousands of relationships to their email list and raised five figures for Untapped Shores.

Case Study: Religious Nonprofit

The Hightshoes' funnel drew in enough visibility and offerings to establish their brand-new church.

As a brand-new congregation, the Hightshoes were having difficulty with the launch budget. They had rented a building but didn't really know how to market themselves. They were on Facebook but needed a way to generate more visibility for the church, serve the community, and grow through donations.

One day, a friend of theirs told them about funnels, but it was hard for them to understand how a sales funnel could change their situation and how it could help them with donations and attendance.

They spent time strategizing and built out a storyboard that would allow conversation and interaction with the community and, finally, a request for donation support.

Especially in years like 2020, where person-to-person connections became almost impossible, creating funnels for attendance, prayer, and donations could keep conversations that led to relationships, faith-building opportunities, and funding alive.

Not only did they survive 2020, but they have thrived and have gathered an online core of 85 people and growing.

Case Study: Community Nonprofit

Carlos Morales's funnel generates funding and volunteers to bring homes and sustainability to an impoverished New Jersey neighborhood!

Carlos was hired as the new executive director of the nonprofit Heart of Camden in New Jersey. When he arrived, they had an outdated website and an enormous task ahead to help the struggling poor by rehabilitating homes and developing new play spaces for the residents in his community.

He had known of Russell Brunson and had read his books. He knew funnels could change his community. Heart of Camden has now built and rehabilitated homes for over 350 Waterfront South families.

Case Study: Instagram

Taylor Thomlinson raised $10,353.53 for the LA Food Bank on her Instagram page in just a couple days.

One of the many people I follow on TikTok, and Instagram is female comedian Taylor Thomlinson. Yes, she can be a bit crude at times, but she is very funny, and I do enjoy her sarcasm. In April 2021, Taylor challenged her online followers to donate to the LA Food Bank, and in just a few days she raised over $10,000 on Instagram alone.

In the years ahead, the marketplace will continue to shift. You and I are a team of treasure hunters. Like a ship running with the shifts in the current, we continue to hunt for the next treasure for our beloved nonprofits. The map of proven digital tools will guide us. The funnels will open the lid on the treasure chest. And "X" marks the spot where you will be standing with the resources to fund your next year!

We're surrounded by new directors saying, "I can raise $25,000; can I raise $50,000?" We have nonprofit founders who have raised over $500,000 and are asking themselves, "Could my team build a million-dollar donor funnel?" We need more visionaries and strategists like them. Who is going to be the next nonprofit to use donor funnels to raise $1 million in one year?

I wonder...
What could you do?

AFTERWORD
WHAT DO I DO NEXT?

I have enjoyed writing this book as much as I hope you have enjoyed reading it. I wanted to answer the question, "What is the new shift in donor acquisition and nonprofit funding?" However, I also wanted to answer, "How does it work?" I hope I have answered these questions for you as well as encouraged you to step into the nonprofit frontier of funnel building and creating digital funding and donor discovery platforms for your nonprofit.

If you have any questions, you can email me at david@nonprofitonline. net. If you are ready to research more on the subject, you can log onto NonprofitOnline.net and look at the options to download free books and other educational and coaching courses.

If you are ready to build your first funnel and engage the laws of e-commerce revenue for your nonprofit's benefit, let us be your guide. We have free webinars to help get you started and 2-Day challenges for your buildouts as a part of our QuickStart Academy to learn superior driver strategies and Google Ad Grant skills.

The Funnel Edu. Graph suggests possible next steps in your nonprofit's workflow that will pave the way for you to be able to launch a complete online strategy in the next 30 days or so. For every nonprofit leader who has read this book, we provide one free consultation valued at $125 as our way of cheering you on in the next step of your journey. Call us or go online and set a date for your free consultation.

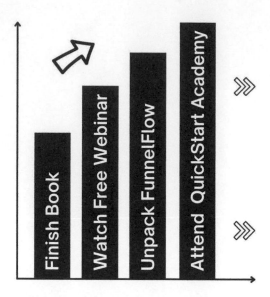

At the very least, let me know how this book spoke to you. I am growing just as you are, and I realize my team and I will still need to uncover many questions and find their answers. I don't mind objections, so if this book frustrated you, I'd love to hear what your frustration was and why. Maybe you see something I don't. Hey, I'm only 50 and way too young to stop learning.

I look forward to connecting with you. Until then, I've got to get back to building the next perfect funnel.

TOOLBOX RECOMMENDATIONS

"You're only as strong as the tools in your toolbox!"

Michael Bastian

Here is a list of my software I recommend...

Category	Program	Cost ($$ less than $99/mo.) Affiliate Link
Design Suite:	Canva	FREE
	Canva Pro	$$
	PlaceIt	$$
Video Storage:	YouTube	FREE
	ClickFunnels 2.0	With March 2022 launch
	Vimeo	$$
Doman Name:	Go Daddy	$
	Namecheap	$
	Google Domains	$

Website Creator:	The Perfect Website - Built by Nonprofit Online for the Google Ad Grant	
	WordPress	$$
	Wix/Squarespace	$$
Email Automation:	ClickFunnels 2.0	FREE (With Premium Subscription) March 2022
	Active Campaign	$$$
Calendaring:	Calendly	$$
Online Sales Site:	ClickFunnels 2.0	FREE (With Premium Subscription) March 2022
	SamCart	$$
Sales Funnel Creator:	ClickFunnels	$$
Webinar Platforms:	ClickFunnels 2.0	$$
	Zoom	$$
CRM:	ClickFunnels 2.0	FREE (With Subscription)
	ZOHO	$$
Texting & Phone:	ClickFunnels 2.0	SS
	DialPad	SS
Automation:	ClickFunnels 2.0	FREE (With Premium Subscription) March 2022
	Zapier	$$
Photography	Canva Pro	$$
	Shutterstock	$$
Flow Mapping:	Funnelytics	$$
Lead Searches	GetProspect	FREE
	D7 Lead Finder	$$

ENDNOTES

"History is the transformation of tumultuous conquerors
into silent endnotes."

—Paul Eldridge

Preface

a. Source: ClickFunnels.com, "Tyler Is Building His Non-Profit Organization, Just Like You", https://goto.clickfunnels.com/nonprofit (accessed May 4, 2021)

Chapter 1

1. Article by Maryam Mohsin, "How Many People Shop Online In 2021", *oberlo.com*, https://www.oberlo.com/statistics/how-many-people-shop-online (accessed June 20 2021)

Chapter 2

2. Article by Katrina Kirsch, "The Ultimate List of Email Marketing Stats for 2021", *blog.hubspot.com*, https://blog.hubspot.com/marketing/email-marketing -stats, Originally published August 13, 2021, updated August 13 2021, (accessed May 14, 2021)

3. Article by Maryam Mohsin, "How Many People Shop Online In 2021", *oberlo.com*, https://www.oberlo.com/statistics/how-many-people-shop-online (accessed Jun 20, 2021)

4. Produced By Nonprofit Tech for Good, "Global NGO Technology Report 2019" *funraise.org*, download at https://www.funraise.org/techreport

5. Produced By Nonprofit Tech for Good, "Global NGO Technology Report 2019" *funraise.org*, download at https://www.funraise.org/techreport

6. Produced By PPRO, "The Local Payment Culture", *ppro.com*, https://www.ppro.com/north-america/.(accessed June 24, 2021)

7. Written by Janessa Lantz, The Five Indicators of Breakout Ecommerce Growth", *blog.rjmetrics.com*, https://blog.rjmetrics.com/2015/02/04/the-five-indicators-of-breakout-ecommerce-growth/, Originally published February 4, 2015 (accessed Jun 12, 2021)

8. Source: Digital Commerce 360, U.S. Department of Commerce; updated January 2021, "US ecommerce grows 44.0% in 2020" *digitalcommerce360.com*, https://www.digitalcommerce360.com/article/us-ecommerce-sales/, Published January 29, 2021 (Accessed May 17, 2021)

9. Source: charity:water, "Meet the Founder" *charitywater.org* https://www.charitywater.org/about/scott-harrison-story, (accessed July 5, 2021)

Chapter 3

10. Source: NP Source, "Charitable Giving Demographics for Nonprofits", *nonprofitssource.com*, https://nonprofitssource.com/online-giving-statistics/demographics/ (accessed June 12, 2021)

11. Written by Radhika Duggal - Forbes Councils Member, "The Key To A Marketer's Success: Understanding Consumer Motivations" *forbes.com*, https://www.forbes.com/sites/forbescommunicationscouncil/2018/04/19/the-key-to-a-marketers-success-understanding-consumer-motivations/?sh=6cd6466971ee (accessed June 9, 2021)

12. Written by Tatsuya Nakagawa, "15 Quick Ways to Create Value and Make a Positive Impression", *lifehack.org*, https://www.lifehack.org/articles/featured/15-quick-ways-to-give-value-and-make-a-positive-impression.html (accessed June 9, 2021)

Chapter 4

13. Written by Benyamin Elias, "Know Your Audience is a Lie But it Still Matters", *activecampaign.com*, https://www.activecampaign.com/blog/know-your-audience, Originally published February 14, 2021, (accessed June 12, 2021)

14. Written by **Joanna Wiebe, "I Explain and Demonstrate Amazon Review Mining for Copywriting"**, *copyhackers.com*, https://copyhackers.com/2014/10/amazon-review-mining/ (accessed June 18,2021) 14b. Source: Merriam-Webster dictionary/ "Definition of *demographic* (Entry 2 of 2) sociology", *merriam-webster*

.com, https://www.merriam-webster.com/dictionary/demographics (accessed June 12, 2021)

15. Written by Dale Odeyemi, "10 Copywriting Secrets That Convert" *slide-share.net*, https://www.slideshare.net/DaleOdeyemi/10-copywriting-secrets-that-convert, Originally published January 3, 2020 (accessed June 18, 2021)

16. Written by Benyamin Elias, "What Is Conversational Marketing? Does It Really Matter, and How Can You Do it Well?", *activecampaign.com*, https://www.activecampaign.com/blog/what-is-conversational-marketing, Originally published October 8, 2018 (accessed June 11, 2021)

Chapter 10

17. Written by Russell Brunson, "Traffic Secrets", Published by Hay House USA, *hayhouse*.com, 2020, Chapter 5/Pages 87-88

18. Written by Pamela Nelly, "The Email List Building Nemesis: Churn Rate", *getresponse.com*, https://www.getresponse.com/blog/email-list-building-nemesis-churn-rate, Originally published February 12, 2015 (accessed July 1, 2021)

Chapter 12

19. Written by Mark Walker-Ford, "The 8 Best Social Media Platforms to Market your Business in 2021" *socialmediatoday.com*, https://www.socialmediatoday.com/news/the-8-best-social-media-platforms-to-market-your-business-in-2021-infograp/595834/, Published February 28, 2021(accessed June 11, 2021)

Chapter 14

20. Source: ClickFunnels.com, "Tyler Is Building His Non-Profit Organization, Just Like You", https://goto.clickfunnels.com/nonprofit (accessed May 4, 2021)

ACKNOWLEDGEMENTS
"MANY HANDS DO MAKE LIGHT WORK"

Thank you to those who helped me write this book.

Dawn, Michelle, Kathy, and Kathy, who pre-read each chapter for flow and connection.

Trisha Gooch—You are an incredible master editor, and I highly recommend you to any of my friends who are writers. You can find Trisha at https:// www.goochwords.com

Bryan Heathman and the Made For Success Publishing team. I understand why Zig Ziglar worked with you to print his work. You are amazing, professional, and strategic at what you do. Thank you for choosing to work with this manuscript and turn it into the book that it is.

ABOUT THE AUTHOR
HE WAS BORN WHERE?

J ust like an adventurer, David Higgins was born on an island in the South Pacific. The county hospital in Palmerston North, New Zealand, was the place where his nonprofit adventure started. The first words he uttered were rumored to be "donor," not "Dada."

Soon after, his family moved to Perth, Australia. His father launched a new group of nonprofits that are still serving the community today. After a short stop back in Auckland to work with a nonprofit on the North Shore, the really big move happened.

In 1978, David and his family came to Washington State and then moved to California where, between that time and his father's passing in 2012, they worked together to launch hundreds of independent nonprofits in the U.S., Europe, Asia, Africa, and the South Pacific. While his father traveled the world inspiring local people and groups to educate and help their populations, he often left David to discover the funding.

Since 2008, much of David's time has been spent in consulting for nonprofits, and this led to the opportunity to launch his greatest nonprofit "heart project," the San Diego Performing Arts Center. In his final year with the PAC, it was providing 2,000 music and dance lessons a week.

The following two years were quiet until David and Michelle moved to Portland, Oregon, to help his brother Seth launch a nonprofit which helps prisoners recently released from incarceration adjust into society, as well as serves as a much-needed food pantry.

Now David and Michelle reside in Yakima, Wash., close to their children and family. To his great joy, two of their sons live in San Diego, which provides many reasons to go to the beach, dreaming of the next amazing nonprofit.

David Higgins is the founder and CEO of Nonprofit Online & Targeted Marketing Group.

For more information go to www.NonprofitOnline.net or email David at david@nonprofitonline.net

Visit Nonprofit Online's YouTube Channel and hit "Like" and "Subscribe" to get updates on the latest in fundraising successes. Also, connect with Nonprofit Online on Facebook, LinkedIn, Twitter, and Instagram.